Faith,

Hope,

Believe

One Woman's Story

M ICHELLE R OSE

BALBOA.
PRESS
A DIVISION OF HAY HOUSE

Balboa Press books may be ordered through booksellers or by contacting:

Balboa Press
A Division of Hay House
1663 Liberty Drive
Bloomington, IN 47403
www.balboapress.com
1 (877) 407-4847

Print information available on the last page.

ISBN: 978-1-9822-0763-2 (sc)
ISBN: 978-1-9822-0765-6 (hc)
ISBN: 978-1-9822-0764-9 (e)

Library of Congress Control Number: 2018908050

Balboa Press rev. date: 07/20/2018

My thoughts, prayers and love go out to anyone who is struggling with any sort of mental illness. This book is dedicated for you.

Prologue

I t's been a year and half since I began to write, I have changed words, added, omitted sentences and deleted pages all together. I question whether what I wrote will be of any value to people out there in the world and yet something inside me tells me that it will.

Can a business women become a writer? Can it happen because I chose to follow a path that was less than ideal to the people all around me? I believe it can, I believe it will. This newfound appreciation and power within me, mental images that only I can see, have given me the courage to try new things and go outside my comfort zone. This journey has allowed me to rediscover who I really am and perhaps who I should have been years ago.

I will never turn back, I will continue on this journey and lead the life I was meant to live. I feel with every part of my inner soul I have taken a turn that was intended for me, a road that I likely would not have attempted had I not re-evaluated my life.

This is the new me, the more profound me, the writer in me. All of these things I did not know existed within me and yet here I am shouting it from the rooftop. This is the new me. I'm following what my true inner-self is telling me. I had reservations, judgments and doubts from others, but I decided to follow what I feel is right. Many told me I was wrong in quitting a job that I once thought of as a career, many didn't have faith, many questioned if my mental state was okay. However, to this day, eighteen months from when it began, I still have complete faith and I know beyond a shadow of a doubt that I am doing what I meant to do at this very moment. It's an incredible feeling, I have no idea where this journey will lead to, but something inside me says it's meant to be. I'm paying attention to everything around me. Some would call these, "coincidences," I call it signs from above that are guiding and leading me to my new purpose.

This book, this journey, the road that I wasn't sure where it was leading me, all began because of our dear friends daughter who died by suicide, a tragic life that was taken away much too soon, a life that should be here today. This journey, my journey began because of her. Your pain, which lead to you final decision, is what forced me to face my pain and perhaps my child's pain.

My journey, my writing began as a way to express my feelings, to make change in the community. To honour anyone who suffers from depression, anxiety and/or mental illness. These were the reasons why I began to write when I didn't know I could write. I wrote so I could make a shout out to the community, the Ministry of Health, the province of Ontario, the Government of Canada to give us more funding in our communities so we can support the well-being of our youth, to ensure the health of our future. Teen suicides continue to increase and we can't let it continue. Our voices need to come together and take a stand. I began to write, to make change, to change our healthcare system. Help each and every individual to know that they don't have to suffer internally; there is joy, love, and hope. We can help; we all can help together.

My goal still remains the same; my focus is to draw awareness and to produce funds to help our teens and young adults. However, somewhere during this journey, somewhere along my writing I became just that, I became a writer. A passion I didn't know I had, a passion I didn't know I enjoyed. I have changed so much along this journey, this past year. I'm a different person, a person now that cherishes every waking day that God has offered me. I have always been grateful for the family and friends that I have been blessed with, but now more than ever; I cherish each and every moment I have with them.

And so, I will continue to work hard, be dedicated and passionate, but now that passion, that dedication, will only encompass what's important to my family, friends and the wellness of others. Mental Health is important to me and I will work hard to make a difference because I am dedicated to doing so. My passion now lies in writing and so I am now excited about what lies ahead for me in this journey we call life. I have changed in ways I couldn't have even dreamed about only a couple years ago. But I am grateful beyond belief, grateful that I have been given this opportunity to change.

I will admit that when I began to write in 2016 there was a lot of anger inside me. I felt as though the entire healthcare system was at fault for how my child was treated. I believed the type of treatment that was given could have potentially altered the outcome of our entire lives. I was full of anger. During this journey I have realized that the entire health care system wasn't to blame. It was a series of unfortunate events that lead down an unwanted road. I now realize that our healthcare system and the staff are working hard to support their patients, but funding, lack of resources, stigma are just some examples of why our system sometimes fails us. I have faith that together we can make a stand, collaborate and work together as a community and help the well-being of our future.

I am not a medical person or expert, the story that lies ahead is my personal experience and solely my thoughts and opinions.

"Save me, I'm lost
Oh lord, I've been waiting for you
I'll pay any cost
Save me from being confused
Show me what I'm looking for
Show me what I'm looking for, oh lord"

Lryics from "Show me what I'm
looking for" by Carolina Liar

Introduction

I hope to teach, inspire, motivate and empower some of you with some of the experiences that I have had. I decided to share what I have learned over the years to hopefully help you.

I hope that one day with some of the proceeds I attain from what I have to say in this book will draw more awareness to mental health, improve the services and programs, and increase coping strategies that we as humans need in order to overcome challenges. Our experiences provide us the opportunity learn and grow from one another and be the best that we can be.

I hope that each one of us can collaborate together and build strength in our teens and young adults' mental wellness, build on our future.

Sadly, as I finished my last chapter another teen suicide occurred in our community last night, two this week, five or six in the past fourteen months (that I am aware of). My heart aches that I have lost count of the tragic deaths in our community. As I write these last few words, I have tears shedding for the families who have to endure the pain that I kept inside me for years as a surviving family member. My heartaches for anyone who is suffering at this present moment, please know that life is worth living.

If you are reading this and at a crossroads in life, please reach out for help, there are services and/or programs that can help you.

If you are reading this and struggling with depression, anxiety, suicidal thoughts, please think twice. This is the aftermath after you are gone. You are special in every sense of the word. Your family and friends need you more than you can ever imagine. Believe in yourself, YOU CAN OVERCOME THIS. You can do this. Reach out to anyone and talk, it's the best step in the right direction. You are loved.

From the beginning we teach our children to never give up. Starting as young as toddlers, if they fall we teach them to get back up and try again. We teach them to keep going. We know that babies, children will learn to crawl, walk, eat, and be self sufficient. We need to continue to support our teens and young adults and teach them that it's ok to fall down. We are here to listen to what you need from us, we will help you pick yourself back up and you will be ok. We need to take the time not only to teach healthy coping strategies to our teens and young adults but also teach and reassure parents that we are all in this together. That parents do have the skills they need to help and guide their children and if they need assistance our healthcare system will be right beside them picking them up and helping to guide them. In my opinion, our healthcare system needs improvement. They need to understand what they are doing now is not working. Changes need to be made.

Parents can no longer live in fear, fear in not knowing what to do next and question every parenting skill they ever knew. Teens and young adults need to know it's ok to feel vulnerable, scared and unsure of life. It's ok that life isn't perfect. We need to teach these individuals, because as a society, we have coddled them and now they can no longer cope with challenges. We need to assure them that the feelings they are having are sometimes NORMAL! Teen years and young adult years are the most frightening time of our lives and also the most important time for our brain to grow. We have to come together to support our healthcare system, ensure that proper guidance is provided to teens, young adults and to parents when they are in crisis. We can create an environment that will empower those of our future. I hope that my words, my thoughts and with the support of others we can and we will stand together and make a difference. I have faith, hope, and believe that our communities will come together and build a solid foundation for children who have just fallen once again and just need encouragement, assurance and support from others to get back up.

When my writing began

A year and half ago, my life got flipped in a direction that I could have never prepared for. My child was struggling with mental health and suddenly our family went into crisis. Our experience was traumatic to say the least. The lack of compassion and empathy I felt from our mental health services was offensive. Teenage years can be tough years. Trying to understand who to be, where to go, and what's the next path in life. Add hormones into the mix, and these children are lost beyond belief. Tackle on devastations such as teen suicides, relationship breakups, educational demands, and the chaotic social web world (where a "like" means everything to their self-image) of course our children are going to have struggles. They are going to have moments of stress, depression and anxiety, wouldn't we all in these circumstances? Why did I feel as though our healthcare system casted immediate judgment on our family and the environment within? Why wasn't our healthcare system teaching our children, youth and young adults the coping strategies that as human beings we all need in order to live through life's challenges? These were the questions that filled me with rage as I began to write.

We as parents, teachers, and health care providers can't prevent terrible things from happening to our children, but we can help them cope. Provide strategies to help them overcome and learn and grow from their experiences. I felt it was wrong when our healthcare system immediately medicated and isolated human beings in individual rooms to eat, read and think by themselves when their self-image is at their lowest.

This is why I am here today, this is why I am writing my story and this is why I am on my new mission. To advocate and ensure young human beings receive the mental health care that they deserve. More importantly, teach them that there are coping strategies that help overcome life's obstacles and challenges. We have it in all of us. We can overcome our crossroads in life. Is medication sometimes required to help us, to guide us? I'm sure in some cases it is. I'm not a Doctor and I am not insinuating that medication is not a solution; however, I was surprised to find out our children and youth are given medication almost immediately after they proclaim they are sad and depressed. Lead to believe that pills are required to get them through their "tough" times in life. There are no beginning stages, no strategies in place before a decision is made to medicate. Why did I not witness an encouragement to socializing, positive thinking, exercise, healthy eating, vitamins, yoga, meditation, connecting with loved ones? As humans we crave love, compassion and affection. Yet, it in my experience our healthcare system decided to isolate our adolescent and young adults at their lowest points.

I'm taking action for everyone who needs someone to take a stand for them. I have heard many stories from families who have children/youth struggling with mental health and they have all said the same thing. The mental health care system is less than ideal (and that's me paraphrasing).

I am writing today, to hopefully make a difference to you and to many others. I hope that some of my experiences and what I have written throughout this book will help and guide you to a better you.

I am here to tell you a bit of my story and how I came to be today. It was an experience that I would never want to go through again; however, it was an experience that has changed me to now live my life to its fullest.

The journey that got me to where I am today was beyond difficult. There were days where I felt alone, afraid, angry, lost and exhausted. However, it was those fears and pain that have lead me to the fulfillment that I feel today. My focus for all of this is to draw awareness to mental health and provide some hope to those of you who need it.

My book is divided into three parts. First, it explains some of my past experiences, challenges, obstacles that I have been faced with. In no way am I trying to indicate that my past challenges are worse or more difficult than what you have experienced in your past. My reasoning is so that you can have an understanding of where I have been. The second part is my transformational moment, the moment I became self aware of who I am today. Lastly, I will end with my coping strategies that have worked for me at my most trying times.

I hope that what I write will provide you some information that you can take and utilize. I hope that it will inspire, motivate and empower you to take action in your own life. I hope to make positive change in mental wellness.

Thank you, for taking the time in reading my story.

"What about us?

What about all the times you said you had the answers?
What about us?
What about all the broken happy ever after's?
What about us?
What about all the plans that ended in disaster?
What about love? What about trust?
What about us?"

Lyrics from "What about us" by Pink

PART 1

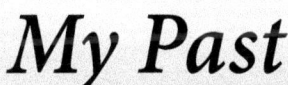

My Past

Chapter

1

Then He Was Gone

L et me take you back to 1990, when there was no such thing as smart phones or social media. A time when Sundays were considered family time and retail stores were rarely open. Yes, those were the simpler days and the times that many of us consider fond memories. Those were the days that we sometimes wish we could all go back to. Music was less about sex and drugs and more about life. Communication was not done through texting and emails but through face-to-face interaction or by telephone. A time when you didn't have to pay so much money for organic foods because we just would go to our local farmers (which were always around the corner) and pick our own fruits and vegetables. Yes, those were the days. Faith was very important in our family. I was raised in a small town in Ontario, Canada. I came from a European background where our traditions and our Catholic religious beliefs were very important. Family gatherings were always a Sunday tradition. Our Sunday's consisted of mass followed by dinner at our Grandparents house where there would be an abundance of food, drinks, and laughs. Our family was loud and obnoxious at times. Laughter sometimes transferred to an argument as my family members battled over a card game, but I loved every moment of it. April 29, 1990 was when that all changed for me and would never be the same again. My mother, siblings and I were at the hospital when I heard the devastation of what suddenly became my reality. A stranger escorted my siblings and I into a separate room. I looked back at my mom and wondered where they were taking us. She looked helpless. As we walked towards a room, something in me felt so strange, something wrong happened. The sudden sounds of my extended family members yelling and crying in hysterics became like a concert in my ears. It's all I heard, it's all I could remember as I was directed into an unknown room for reasons I was about to find out. There was a woman sitting there, waiting for our arrival. Although I can't recall what she looked liked, I do remember the words that came out of *my* mouth. "My dad is gone, isn't he?" I can't begin to explain to you, how or why I said what I said that day but everything inside me told me that I was right. The counselor before me, shook her head yes. I ran to her for a hug that I so desperately needed. I was twelve when I found out that my father died by suicide. It's hard to explain the emotions that one goes through when a child loses a parent, especially when they die by suicide.

Chapter 2

Suicide, What does that mean?

L ost, anger, confused, blame, shame are just a few of many emotions that ran through my body almost daily for years to follow. My family, being as religious as they were and going back in the 1990s mental health and/or mental illness was never talked about. Back then; the stigma against mental illness was far from positive. After my father had passed, reasoning for his death began to be spoken in a way that was all too confusing to me. I heard many things such as the devil was with him, our family had a curse, evil took over him, he will not go into heaven until it was his actual time to go (which meant he roamed around the earth until it was his time). These were just a few of many things that I was told. At twelve I didn't know what mental illness was nor did I hear the word "stigma" or "suicide" before; however, one thing I did know was that I chose not to believe anything that I was hearing. Something didn't seem to be true, none of it made sense to me even at twelve. My father's death brought the worst out in people, his funeral (and now my memories) included yelling, blaming, and family members be escorted out. It was devastating to watch, with what was already a horrific situation. After that horrible day, my siblings, my mother and I walked away from my extended family and continued our lives the best we could.

I was fifteen when I made the choice to move out of our families home. Not because I didn't have all the necessities that I needed but because I just felt like I had too. I was mad, I was mad at the world. I was mad at my father who chose to die, I was mad at my extended family who made my father's funeral a three ring circus and more importantly I was mad at myself. I could have saved my father, if I was there that day, if I was with him. I promised him I would never leave him, yet I did. "Why did I lie to my father?" "Maybe he would still be alive had I kept my promise". These are just a few statements, questions that ran through my head constantly during my teenage years.

Chapter 3

Fifteen, lost and determined

Here I was fifteen, made the decision to move away from home at a time that was questionably the most pivotal time of my life. Like many teens I thought I could handle it, I thought I was strong and more importantly I thought I was independent enough that life away from home was the right decision for me. As a teenager life is tough as it is. Trying to discover who I was, who I wanted to be, and who I was definitely not going to be. Being a child with a father who died from suicide and then decided to move out at fifteen, well, as you can imagine judgments were made. None were ever spoken, but I could always see it in people's faces when I looked into there eyes. Their sympathy, their pity, their judgments, their assumptions, I could see and feel it all. It was clear that many thought I wasn't going to make much of myself, but what did they know. I was going to overcome this. I was still very much in pain, I was hurting inside and I was lost in more ways than I could have imagined, but I was going to prove to myself and others that I was going to move pass from this.

At the time, I was determined to make something of myself despite the sadness and fear within me. Life was hard, I struggled internally with my emotions; although, I rarely expressed them. I lost my father at twelve, talked myself into believing that there were countless ways that I could have saved him and yet I didn't. For years following I internalized my own blame, sadness, guilt and shame. I blamed myself for years as a teen. Eventually, I told myself that I had to block out my past, bury it so no one knows my true past. I ignored the reality, and just moved on. So, that's what I choose to do. To move forward with what life had in store with little acceptance of what my past life consisted of.

Fifteen, Sixteen, Seventeen the teen years, negative temptations all around me, a time when I had no idea who I was and trying to discover the person I wanted to become. There wasn't the chaos of opium's and the level of drugs like today, but there were certainly temptations. Alcohol and drugs such as acid, ecstasy and mushrooms were around me. I struggled a lot, I still had people around that believed and told me that our family had a curse and that our lives would not amount to much (more or less to just accept the reality). And yet, I was destined and determined to prove these individuals wrong. I was surrounded with the "easy way out," I could have skipped school as frequently as I wanted and I could have stayed out as late as I chose, but I didn't. Something inside told me otherwise. I can't explain it, I still needed to stay true to who I really was, who I wanted to be. I felt like I needed to prove to anyone who knew me that I was going to make it. That I was going to reach every goal that I had set out for myself.

Grade 9, I was the ideal student, good grades, listened to the teacher, "teacher's pet" as they called it back in the day. Then what seemed to come like a bolt of lightening, the hormones entered with a vengeance. I went from a confident, strong willed young teen to a lost and angry teen. I didn't know what happened. Suddenly, trying to figure out who I wanted to be and where I was going to fit in, in this world, we call high school seemed difficult. Yes, there were days that inside I was hurting beyond belief but no one exterior would ever know the pain or the hurt I was feeling. I had to move past it. I had to leave the pain tucked away. Here I was living on my own in a small basement apartment, afraid of what my future would look like. How I was going to get there? The friendships I created during my high school days were wonderful. I finally felt like I fit in somewhere, felt like I had people who helped me pretend (although they didn't know it) that my life from my past didn't exist. I lost my ways as I headed into the senior years of high school. I drank, did "some" drugs and started skipping school. My choices were beginning to lead down a road that I knew I didn't want to go down. Thankfully, these temptations never took the best of me. Although I was lost, there was always a part of me that reminded me to keep it together. I had job that helped me stay on track. I worked hard; I got a job at a fish/chip restaurant where I made enough money to cover my costs for living. Suddenly I found myself working instead of studying, my grades were dropping but my job skills were getting stronger. I wondered whether I was making the right decision but it's the choice I decided to make. I slowly became, less the ideal student and more the dependable employee. I never thought about giving up on school; it wasn't an option for me. I knew I had to finish; I had to prove to myself that I could do this. I felt as though I had to prove to others that my life was not going to become the "statistic," (I told myself that almost daily). My years as a teen, I learned to take that "noise" (the assumptions of others that I felt I was surrounded by) and throw it out the window where it was just a slight whisper, where I could recall it and use it as ammunition to continue on my journey to make something of myself. My pain inside was being expressed in less than ideal ways, drinking and skipping school. I felt like I had no control over it. How did this happen? How was I letting myself continue on this path when everything inside me was telling me this is wrong? Why? I realized I was really losing who I was, who I wanted to be. A strong, determined, and well managed teen that knew with every part of her being that she was going to be fine. Suddenly I wasn't.

Chapter 4

Friendship turns to Family

M y close friend who I cherished since grade school suddenly welcomed me into her home. Her family welcomed me with open arms. I never found out why they took me in. Maybe deep down they knew I had begun to fall apart or that I was losing sight of who I wanted to become. Maybe it was from the years of friendship. The answer remains a mystery to me, but I will forever be grateful. This family was like a second family to me at a young age. A family that I often would pray that I was a part of it because they were "normal." I desperately wanted a father, mother and siblings sitting at a dinner table playing card games and chatting about sports and school. They had everything I wanted. I didn't want the fancy cars, the fancy clothes, the fancy trips I wanted a family to sit at a table and play cards with, but I didn't have it. This family who welcomed me into their home for most of my high school life meant everything to me. Each one of them took part in helping and guiding me back to the person I wanted to be. Guided me back to the fundamentals that I needed. They helped me get a job at Burger King where I continued to work hard and eventually earned my way to late night manager. This family reminded me that staying focused on what I want in life could happen. They reminded me that the road that I was headed was not the road I wanted to continue on. My life began to seem clearer again, my visions and aspirations became more focused. "I got this, don't lose focus, this is the road that is going to lead you to the road of success." And so I continued on my road to success. There were still many days were I would cry in my room, where I would feel lost and confused but there were still days that I felt strong, determined, and proud of myself. The days where I felt strong and determined were the days I clung to and re-energized myself. I clung onto the days that I felt confident, determined, and assured that life is good. The days when I felt that God was leading me in the direction that I was meant to be lead. During my teen years, I worked a lot, I enjoyed it and I learned so much. I continued to tell myself that I am capable, no matter what task was given to me. I CAN do whatever I set my mind too.

5

College life and Suppression

I finished high school; I was finally done with the chaos. I completed high school in less than ideal grades but; nevertheless, I stayed on task and completed the road I wanted to finish. Then I was off to college. Taking business administration, working at a bank was my goal. The goal I knew I wanted since the age of seven. I moved in with a couple of wonderful friends and then we headed onto the next chapter, which was the college journey. What a journey that was.

What do people think of when they think of college? I think about studying, higher education, parties, drinking and still trying to figure who we really are. Those years were wonderful. Had a blast living the college life, living with friends, connecting with new people. It was great. I was in college, making something of myself and living with two roommates' who were perfect for my social circle. My past became more of a distant memory. I look back now and realized I tried to believe it didn't even exist. Many didn't know the real reason how or why my father passed and I intended to keep it that way. I chose to block it out, for me, I thought it was the right decision. I didn't want people to believe that I was broken in some way; I wanted people to see the strong individual that I knew I was or talked myself into believing I was. It's what I felt I had to showcase. I still believed in myself, I still believed that although I had my share of struggles, I was not going to let anything stop me from reaching my goals in life.

My father's death became a thing of the past. I didn't talk about it; I certainly didn't acknowledge it and I never uttered the words, "suicide" or "mental illness". To me, I was ashamed. The stigma and the theories I heard regarding mental illness and suicide were scary to me. Some days they seemed absurd and then other days they seemed rational. Some days I was angry and some days I was grateful. Grateful to be alive, grateful to have family and friends and grateful to always have basic needs met. Eventually, over time my gratitude took precedence over my madness, my hatred, and my anger.

I know look back and realize that although I had gratitude for what I had in life, my feelings of hatred anger were never gone, I unconsciously chose to suppress my feelings.

Chapter

6

My Love Who Waited

At sixteen, I was blessed to meet the man that I was destined to have a life with. A boy who was seventeen, gelled hair, leather coat and a black cutlass enters my life and all I thought was, who is this guy? Who does he think he is? Little did I know that I was going to have a roller coaster relationship with the man that I married eight years later. My husband, the teen boy that use to go to Burger King daily and buy a whopper just to see me at drive thru was the second half of me that completed the true me. I ran this man thru the ringer, one day I loved him and the next day I didn't. At seventeen, he professed his love for me and told me that he was going to marry me one day. I just laughed and thought it was the funniest thing I had heard in years. Life has a funny way of presenting the gifts you are destined to have. That's what my husband was to me and continues to be. He's a gift, that I have been blessed to have as a part of me for most of my life. He completes me in ways I didn't know I needed to be complete. As teens, we were that couple off and on again, I was less than the ideal girlfriend since majority of the time I had no idea what I wanted from him. And yet, he stayed around, he waited for me, he loved me and he knew we were meant to be. I love him more then words can explain and with every challenge that comes our way, somehow it reunites us. Our life experiences reconnect us and reconfirm out love. My husband was the man that made me trust men again. He loved me at times when I thought I didn't deserve it, but I am grateful beyond belief that he waited.

Chapter 7

Our family of three was Wonderful

That fateful day when my daughter was born, August 5, 1999 she changed my life in ways I that I never imagined. She made me appreciate the finer things in life each and every day. I loved holidays once again. Since my father's death, I could have cared less for holidays. She instantly changed me into a better person, she taught me so much in seconds upon her arrival. For her, I will always be eternally grateful. It was my daughter that made me realize life is something special. Life always has purpose and meaning. Life is always worth living for. I was more determined than ever to make a difference now. I had someone who looked up to me, who I needed to show that the world is a beautiful place and not a horrible place. I was determined to make her life special and filled with love.

At a young age I had always envisioned working at a financial institution. It was a career that I found fascinating and looked enjoyable. Now, at twenty-one I was determined to work at one of the banks because now I have a child. A child who deserves a wonderful life, a life filled with joy, happiness and all the finer things in life. That was my next challenge. Continuing my education and getting a career that I was proud of and a career that will help support our family. I went out and handed resumes to every bank in our city: monthly, sometimes weekly. Nothing was going to stop me from becoming known in the financial industry. After several months of handing out resumes and days where I thought I was ready to give up. I got, "the call". It was amazing. It once again proved to me that If I'm determined and dedicated enough, I can achieve what I want. My life was wonderful. I had an amazing husband, a beautiful baby girl, and a career that I was proud of.

Chapter 8

Four became Six

Fast forward five years and we welcomed our newest addition to our family, our little boy. Anyone, who has become a parent can relate to the feelings and love that instantly take over your body each and every time you welcome a child into the world. Those moments are incredible and life changing. Here we were a family of four. Both had good paying, respectable jobs, a wonderful family, and a beautiful home. We couldn't ask for more. Life was great; I had everything I had worked so hard for. In my mind, I proved all those individuals wrong, those who judged me, who believed that I wouldn't make anything of myself, and those who spoke of me in negative ways. Individuals that didn't support me, chose to speak poor of me, believed that I was going to be a failure, I stayed away from. That negative energy is never good for anyone. I got to where I was by surrounding myself with individuals who helped me stay on task, believed in me and supported me. Those are the people that helped me get to the life that I achieved.

Another five years goes by and life took another turn. My husband, my children and I just got back from our first "real" family vacation in Florida. My sister in-law was a wonderful woman, who suffered from diabetes and was born with a heart condition. Between my mother in-law and my sister in-law we were accustomed to unexpected hospital visits. None of us thought anything different when she called and told us she was heading to the hospital because she didn't feel well. That evening we received a call by the doctor; she was fine but that they were going to keep her for observation overnight. The very next morning, we got a call to rush to the hospital because she wasn't doing well. Within forty-eight hours, she had passed. April 27, 2010, it was quick, that none of us really comprehended what had happened. She was a single mom of two teenage boys and all of a sudden she was gone. Her husband and her, separated when the boys were ages two and three. Her ex-husband lived three hours away from our hometown. My two nephews lost a parent, something I understood, and feelings I could relate to all too well. My in-laws needed me, they had suddenly lost their daughter, they were falling apart. My husband who lost his sibling and my children who lost their aunt; I had to help my family, they all needed me. Life seemed like a active tornado at that time. I felt as though I had to be at ten different places and all at the same time. My two nephews who I've watched grown into two wonderful teenagers, lost their mother and now wanted to live with us. I'll never forget the day, when my husband came home and said, "The boys want to live with us, how do you feel about it?" There was no doubt in my mind; we definitely were going to take care of my nephews. They were fifteen and sixteen at the time, lost a parent and wanted to come live with my husband and I. How could I say no? How could anyone say no? So, it was settled. My husband quickly had to finish our basement and make two additional bedrooms for our newest addition to our family. I kept going in circles between each of the family members and making sure that everyone was ok. I felt horrible for my husband; he couldn't allow himself the time to grieve. Getting the basement ready for the boys took all of his time after work. He worked so hard; to make sure they were going to feel as comfortable as possible. Just like that, we became a family of six. Life was hectic to say the least. Learning to raise not one but two teenage children who were both grieving, while also raising my ten and five year old children who were also grieving was a challenge. It took months to really find our rhythm and how our new family was going to work together. I continued to bounce between the four children, my husband, and my in-laws. I felt this desperate need to make sure that everyone was doing ok and that I was there to help them when they needed me. In my mind, I was handling it. I was tired, but I was handling it. Until six months later. It's like I hit a wall. It was that sudden. I sat and cried for hours and for days about everything and anything. How can I be there for everyone? How can I help my two nephews who so desperately want their mother back? How can I help my two children who are dealing with so many changes all at the same time? How can I continue to help my in-laws as frequently as I do? How can I support my husband?

I couldn't. I couldn't do it anymore. I gave every ounce of my energy to everyone else and forgot about me. I was advised by many to take a few weeks off work and adjust, figure me out, and help my family. So, I did just that. I took five weeks off and in that time, while the kids were at school, I spent a lot of alone time. Reflecting on what happened, trying to understand what happened and why? I walked, just to help me think. Help me think rationally. I read a lot of self-help books. I had wonderful friends who knew just the right time when I needed a night out with the girls. Surprisingly, one of the main things that helped me cope and move forward was laughter. More specifically Ellen DeGeneres. I watched her show daily; it was the one-hour that I could remove myself from my life and just laugh. Laughter is beyond therapeutic; it's what I quickly realized was the strategy that was going to help me get back on track. I have always lived a life of determination, dedication and positive thinking. I had to readjust and get back on that track. Self-help books, walks in nature, surrounding myself with friends and family, and The Ellen DeGeneres Show were going to help me get there again. Over those short weeks, I did get stronger and better every day. Life was making sense once again; I understood what my next challenge in life was going to be. I was ready to take it on, ready to raise my four children. I'd like to tell you it got simpler, but anyone who has children knows it never does. It only gets more complicated and challenging; however, the love and bond that we created with the six of us was powerful. Our family took on an unexpected twist but in the end it made all of us stronger, thankful and appreciate the most important things in life. The four kids became so close, and I gained two more children. It was never my intent to replace my sister in-law, their mom, but my sole purpose was to help guide, love and nourish those boys. The love that I developed for them was no different than the love I had for my two youngest children.

Chapter 9

Yellow Hurts

Shortly after our family became a family of six our small community was having a trailing effect of teen suicides. I was surrounded by it and yet couldn't acknowledge it. I had spent the majority of my life pretending, avoiding the reality of my father's death and now all of a sudden it's everywhere I turned. Family, friends, coworkers, and media-it's what everyone was talking about. The devastation that was hitting my family and our community was overwhelming. I remember, the day the residents of our community had decided to make Friday's, "yellow days" in support of suicide awareness. It was the hardest colour to put on for me. A yellow shirt, to many is just that, "a yellow shirt". To me, a yellow shirt signified: devastation, horror, sadness, anger, loss, and fear. All the emotions that I chose to ignore so long ago. Yet, I moved forward, I did once before and I'll do it again. I put on that yellow shirt every Friday for as long as the community wanted because I felt it was the right thing to do. Once again, I returned to self-help books, exercise, friends and family and The Ellen DeGeneres show to help me cope with what was surrounding me.

Everyday I focused on making me stronger, doing the activities that I knew helped me overcome obstacles and challenges that I had lived through in my past. I had learned several different tactics that worked for me and I knew that I was once again determined to move past this and once again enjoy the simple things in life.

A year and a half later our family of six went down to a family five when our oldest nephew went off to college and began his next chapter. We continued on with our day-to-day lives. I progressed in my career, received the promotion that I had always wanted. Life was once again looking up and doing great. My second nephew eventually went off to school as well and began his next chapter in life. I was so proud of those boys. Each of them had there own set of challenges and yet they overcame it with strength and determination. I love them beyond words. I want their lives to be filled with laughter, love, and happiness because that's what they deserve. Isn't that what we all deserve?

Chapter 10

2016

I t seemed like our household went back down to four in a snap of a finger. It was eight years all together but wow does time fly by, years of highs and lows, laughter and cries but most importantly family bond. It was the summer of 2016 when we adjusted back to a household of four, my children now twelve and seventeen. Little did I know that this was also going to be the worst summer of my life thus far. The summer that no one could have prepared us for, it's the year I will never forget.

August 6, 2016 was tragic for our friends, our family and our community. We were left in a state of confusion, deep sadness and utter heartache when we found out that our friends' daughter decided that her only way out of her sadness was to die by suicide. As we were all trying to comprehend what just had happened, trying to make sense of it all it; one week later I found out my child had similar thoughts. There is no way to explain in words the feelings a parent has when a child is suffering with anxiety, depression and any other mental illness. I was lost for days, weeks and months to come. The fear that runs your life is utter horror. There was days that I didn't sleep a wink. Days when I felt as if I was looking down on myself with a bird's eye view. I passed each day trying to understand what was happening. It was strange, it felt as though I was out of my body, staring at myself, asking, what are you going to do? Here I was, a thirty-eight year old mom, trying to be there for our dear friends who lost their daughter in the most horrific way, but more importantly being there for my children. Trying to teach what I believed so strongly about, challenges are hard but we can get through it together and we will. As I tried to understand and figure what my next steps were, I also had to battle my own past, the twelve-year-old child that I buried inside so long ago. I spent years never acknowledging suicide and mental illness out of anger, fear, shame, blame and sadness and yet here I am having it all resurface and at the worst time possible. It seemed as though I was battling with myself. Somehow, someway, I needed to be the mom that could help my children during this devastating time, but also nourish and console the twelve-year-old inside me who was crying out for help so desperately. I went years without saying the word, "suicide." That word, oh that word... it made my heart ache beyond words when I heard it, when I read it and when I saw it. It was the one word in the entire vocabulary that I could not nor would not say. "Suicide", "mental illness", these words were from past, my past that I chose to forget so long ago. Yet now I had no choice, I had to confront the child inside me and deal with my internal pain. My child was suffering and I had to help. For me to help, I had to help myself first. As a parent, you don't realize what your children are seeing, what they understand and what they believe to be true. I never articulated that the word, "suicide" or "mental illness" were "bad" words, yet my avoidance to the subject led them to believe that. For twenty-seven-years, I avoided the word "suicide." The emotional attachment of that word caused to much pain.

A close friend of mine taught me in the power of the word "*yet*". My friend, who is in the school board and well educated in suicide prevention, she gave me books, pamphlets and helped me to understand signs, actions and words that would help me, educate me. Every time I said, "I can't say that word" she came back with the word *"yet."* At the time I thought she didn't make any sense, the word *"yet"* doesn't change anything. It will never make me say it, will never make the heartache stop if I say "the word". Each time I said, "I can't" or "I won't" she finished my sentence with, *"yet"*. I left her house that evening still uneasy but with a little comfort. I went home and talked to my husband about my evening and the lessons and conversation I had with my dear friend. As I was explaining what we were talking about it, I said the word, "suicide". It almost came out automatically but the aftereffect was not that easy. I literally stopped talking, took a deep breath and sat there in silence for several minutes. My husband stood there, I think allowing me the time to understand what had just happened. Although it didn't completely heal all my inner pain, it certainly was a step in the right direction. I couldn't believe it. I said the word. It almost lifted a little weight off my shoulders, which truthfully I didn't know I was carrying. That was when it was clear to me that maybe my friends and family were right. I had some healing from my past that I had to face. The next several weeks felt like an extreme roller coaster. Being a supportive mom to my children was by far the most important; secondly, being the parent to console the twelve-year-old who was aching inside. I used this time to understand, to educate and to heal my past and my present. I took the first step and now I had to keep going.

Chapter 11

One Step at a Time

I was a businesswoman; professional, very factual and I enjoyed living a very structured life. Life was hectic at times. Days, weeks and months always flew by, our schedules were full with work, sports schedules, household chores, emails, text, social media and everything else that needs to get done when you have a family. All of the sudden, EVERYTHING was put on a halt. It was like someone slammed the brakes on our lives and we all had no choice but to stop. We had no choice but to focus on ourselves, on our family and on today.... only today. The future that I once envisioned to be, all of a sudden seemed like a distant memory. The future now seemed like blurry images with no clarity, no absolute certainty, and no confirmation. I was forced to focus on the Now, on the present, because that's all I could do. Some days were unbelievably hard, some days I couldn't get out of bed, some days I cried so hard I couldn't see out of my eyes. There were days I wish I could have slept it all away. Over the course of several weeks, I knew I had to put myself back together again. I needed too, I had too; I had a family who needed me more than anything. I also knew I was falling apart. I started isolating and distancing myself from friends and family. I started to feel alone even though I knew I was surrounded my many wonderful friends and family. I had amazing friends who helped me along this journey. I have know idea how they knew when to just come to my door, when I needed a friend, but they did. They forced themselves in and for that I will forever be grateful.

I took time off work because I knew I had to. I didn't know who I was anymore; I didn't know what I was supposed to do anymore. All I knew was I wanted my family together; healthy (both mentally and physically) and happy. I had to make that happen, I was going to make that happen. I prayed nearly every day for God to give me the guidance and strength to follow what lies ahead. Day by day I felt a sense of relief, a sense of peace that God was protecting my family and me.

But why? Why, would our family be dealt with this situation, this living nightmare? I struggled many days wondering what was the purpose. I needed to find something good out of this horrible situation. I had days where I literally did nothing except relax, not relax my physical body but relax my mental body. I was tired, more tired than any physical thing that I could have done in this world. I knew I needed more time, more time for me to put me back together again. This time I began my healing journey with writing down things I was grateful for. I re-read each one over and over daily. I continued to add to my list everyday. There were days where I was full of anger, grief and sadness. Many days I struggled with trying to find things that filled me with gratitude. I chose to look deep and despite the sadness and pain, there was always something to be grateful for. I continued to write, add to and read my list of grateful things because something inside me believed that this was going to help me in the long haul. I also began to exercise every day not because I wanted too, but because I knew I had to. I never was a faithful gym person, but I knew it was also the right activity to get me out of the isolation that I created for myself. Self-help books, exercise, yoga, prayer, and being grateful became my must-do daily activities. I couldn't continue with what

I was doing anymore. I had to re-focus and move forward. I could feel these daily activities were helping, I was still tired, had days where I was lost and confused but for the most part the activities were helping me. Social media became too hard for me, so I chose to unplug for a few months. I found myself either going one of two ways. The sad and emotional media comments would affect me negatively yet the media comments with "happy family pictures" etc. would anger me. Anger that ultimately was envy inside. Envy that these individuals were living a happy life while mine was a nightmare (even though I knew what we see on social media is never the full truth). After I realized the effect social media was having on me, I made a conscious decision to "unplug" until I was emotionally stronger. All of these things were helping me, helping me get stronger, helping me be the parent and the adult that I once was. As I became more focused, I also become more focused on the now; the beauty of today. When someone is forced to just look at today we tend to realize the beauty that's right in front of our eyes. Before all of this, my life was busy. I never looked at the beauty of our city, the beauty of nature, the beauty of nature sounds. During this life changing moment, transitional moment, aha moment, defining moment whatever the correct terminology is, it happened to me. This moment, this life changing moment was so incredibly powerful, so incredibly monumental, something I will never forget and will never turn back. The glory about this life changing moment, once you have reached it you become consciously aware and know that life can no longer be any other way. Although the transition to this magical time of my life forced me to go through a terrible time, it's changed me in countless ways. The Miracle Book by Rhonda Byrne, I'll forever be grateful to have seen it at the bookstore. It was on that day that everything in my life was going to change for the better, I purchased it primarily to keep me focused, keep me positive and keep me having faith despite the challenges that my family and I were faced with. This horrible tragedy that happened with my friends, with my family, with our community made me stop. Made me have the moment that I realized that life today is more powerful than life from the past or the future. I finally felt at peace with my father's death. It took twenty-seven years for me to feel this way. It took twenty-seven years for me to understand that he was depressed. It took twenty-seven years for me to release the anger and blame.

Chapter 12

A song to remember

My father loved Elvis Presley; there wasn't a time when I could hear any of his songs without leaving the premises or going into a bathroom stall and plugging my ears. There was a song that would often play in church and every time I heard it, I had the sudden urge to cry but never knew why. Until my family was celebrating my child's first communion and the song played, it was then that I remembered the song was played at my father's funeral. I look back now and realize that all of these were signs, triggers and confirmations that I hadn't dealt with my past. However, I believed my behaviours were rational since I had suffered from a loss by suicide. Avoidance of my reality did not work; I needed to accept what had been given to me, good and bad. I didn't believe my present should have been a constant reminder of my past. However, my past was still a part of my story. When I told my story and was at peace, that's when I really enjoyed the present, truthfully enjoyed the gift of now.

Life was beginning to make sense again, my family, all of us were getting stronger, understanding one another and supporting one another. My child made a choice to have received additional support that was needed to help overcome the challenges that were presented, my incredible child although was lost and depressed in many ways still had a sense of determination and commitment to overcome this. I couldn't be more proud. It was then that truly allowed me the time I needed to understand, educate and heal my past and my present.

During our journey with the mental health system, I felt that the services were weak and poorly run. Do I believe that my child was treated unfairly? Do I believe medication was prescribed or given that was much too high or perhaps not needed? Do I believe weeks ahead got terribly worse before they got better because of the medication that was prescribed? Yes, yes and yes!

Initially, the anger came at a vengeance. I was filled with this fire aching pain inside for the lack of respect that was provided to me, my family and more importantly my child. I went to the hospital to state my concerns like a fierce bull ready to charge and tackle anything that came in my way. I was ready to take down the people who I felt hurt us, made assumptions, judged, and lacked empathy. In my mind, I felt that the entire health-care system failed us. I look back now and realize I was wrong.

This experience, wasn't something we asked for, I spent my entire adult life loving and caring for my children. My family was everything to me and yet I felt as though the health-care system made me feel like a failure. I would give up everything and anything for the health, love and happiness for my children. Why did I feel like I was nothing less than someone to blame for the struggles that my child was going through? Why wasn't their support provided to my family and I? Why did I feel so alone?

PART 2

Transformation

Chapter 13

Anger, Fear - make it go away.

Four months past, I began to see the light again. I began to see clearly again and became more of the person I once was. However, this time something was different. I felt clearer than ever, it was as though I had a self-revelation. I understood what my next path in life had to be. After many conversations, and with the support of my spouse we made a decision that going back to my professional career, my comfort zone for the past sixteen years, was going to be a thing of the past. There was a calling for me for something so much more, I made a choice to go into a world of the unknown. Fear? Absolutely! But fear and the unknown I chose to embrace nonetheless. There were many questions that ran through my mind daily: Will my child overcome this? Will my family be all right? Can I make a difference in mental health? Where do I go from here? What actually lies ahead? Still I knew I was starting on the right path.

So, the decision was made. I wasn't going back to work, I was taking a leap of faith that everything was going to work out. Each step ahead would bring me to the next stage and allow me to do amazing things, ensuring the Mental Health System had the awareness it needed. My primary focus was to guide, support, and protect my children and then to develop a plan to ensure there is compassion, empathy and support for those who struggle with mental health.

I had this feeling that I had to become a voice. I had to help make a difference for the youth and families who are affected by mental health. Here I was on my next mission in life, to take a stand for my family and for every family who has needed support in the mental health sector.

I felt as though our health-care system intensified my feelings of shame, blame and guilt, something I was determined to change for others. I felt that there was no support for any of us. How could this be? How could I feel this way?

I have had moments in my past where I wondered; why is this happening? Will it ever change? Will our lives go back to "normal" ever again? In our lives there are times when crisis occurs and you feel helpless in every sense of the word. At times I didn't know if my world was ever going to change. At times I felt like burying myself in a hole to hide from the shame and guilt. BUT (and that's a big but) there came a time when I had to accept the journey that had been given to me and move forward. My experience, my family's experiences lead me down this path. Lead to the journey I am on today and for that I am grateful. Life had been difficult, but now it is so much simpler for me. I am happier than I ever thought I could be. I have moved on from my past that I didn't know I needed to move forward from, and my child is taking the experience and learning and growing and becoming stronger and stronger every single day.

Someone once told me, "As a parent you are only as happy and healthy as your saddest child". I couldn't agree more. I can write this today, I can volunteer, and I can advocate for mental health all because my family is together, healthy and happy.

I'm on this journey for a reason. This experience was nothing less than devastating, but with devastation there needs to be something good that follows. If I allowed life to stand still and allowed my hope to diminish, the anger and pain could have consumed me. I made sure I wouldn't allow that to happen.

I made a promise to my family, my community, and myself. Teens and families who struggle with mental health or any challenge, crisis or devastation deserve support, love, and compassion. They deserved to receive the resources that will help them move on, move forward and begin to heal.

I was terrified and I was angry at the world. I stopped those feelings. I took a look at myself and realized who I was becoming. Life experiences can change you in ways that are less than becoming. It was happening to me. Until one day, I decided it wasn't.

Chapter 14

Except the journey

It's almost like the world just shifted and I saw the reality of what was. My life changed and my family's life changed. I couldn't stop it, I couldn't change it but I could change me. I could change how I presented me. I could show I can make a difference. It's not about stating your concerns in vicious ways, those behaviors gets all of us nowhere. It's about communication, in the most empathetic way. We are here to help one another, to be kind to one another and to support one another. I decided that the only way I can make a difference is by expressing my concerns and ensuring that changes, positive changes, will be made.

The hospital, the place I once believed to be a healing area, was now a place where my darkest memories of anger, shame, guilt, pain, judgments, fear and blame overcame me. I learned to put those feelings aside. I had to help others and the way to do that was to ensure our mental health care system was going to improve.

I made a promise that I intended to keep. I began volunteering in areas where I was able to help others in mental health. Hope that I can help increase awareness in treatment of empathy, compassion and humanity by our healthcare providers. Opportunities to make a difference in the mental health sector were beginning to appear. I was meeting the right people, connections were being made, and suddenly the goals of me helping making a difference were happening almost effortlessly. I became a co-chair to an advisory committee where the family voices and family perspectives were being heard and respected by the health-care system. I was asked to be part of a project at our local hospital to improve the layout and space for our children and youth who needed mental health services. The project focused on ensuring appropriate space was provided to children, youth and their families. Lastly, I was asked to participate in implementing digital stigma reduction curricula to help improve the negative attitudes and behaviours towards mental health patients by healthcare providers (waiting on approval for funding from our Ministry of Health).

Becoming involved and volunteering gave me hope. It helped me understand the healthcare system, the organization and their mission, values and beliefs. I learned to accept that my family's personal experience was not intended. Volunteering allowed me to see things differently, opened me to the understanding that accidents do happen. Humans do make mistakes, and mistakes can be forgiven. That was the path, which lead to my forgiveness. Volunteering and giving back helped me overcome my anger and pain. We all need to forgive. Whatever you have held on too, whether it is your past, family, friends, employment etc. you need to try and find a way to let it go. Forgiveness allowed me to become a better person. I had to let go of the anger.

I think back when I worked at the bank and managed a wonderful group of individuals a couple years ago, and there was this one special woman who struggled at times. She let her past experiences; her assumptions get the best of her. I often told her, "let it go" in the hymn similar to the movie "Frozen." Let it go, it was almost a daily connection her and I had, it seemed to help her. Two years later, and I find myself saying the same thing but this time to me. Let it go.... I had to forgive the staff, the hospital, the experience all-together. I had to forgive and let it go. Once I forgave, a sign of relief overcame every part of your body. I felt at peace, I accepted the experience, embraced it, learned from it and then began looking to make a change for the better.

Chapter *15*

"Things Happen for a Reason"

A common phrase, "Things happen for a reason:" Five words I did not want to hear while I was in a middle of a crisis, but people were compelled to say those words to me. At the time, I couldn't understand or comprehend why this was happening to my family and me. It angered me when people would say, "things happen for a reason." As time passed with each of my experiences, both positive and negative, I realized I have always learned something and grew from it. If anything at all, my life experiences showed the strength, determination and willpower I had within. It was the obstacles, challenges, those "things that happen for a reason" that showed me what I are truly capable of. My life challenges reminded me of the strength I had within, the appreciation of life itself, appreciation that I often took for granted. If this experience had never happened, would I still be the strong, independent, determined individual that I had always been? Yes. Would I still have been an individual who was grateful and appreciated everything I had in life? Yes. Would I still be the adult who would cried in a bathroom stall when I heard Elvis Presley play or cringe with emotion if I heard the word or saw the word, "suicide." Sadly Yes. Would I ever want this experience to happen, absolutely not! BUT, it forced me to face my past. A past that I didn't know needed facing. I didn't realize the burden, the pressure, the feelings I held within me so strong and so deep. This experience forced the twelve year old inside me to cry and to let out. The pain and suffering that was buried for many years. I am finally at peace; my past is finally just my past and only my past. It's part of my story and for the first time ever; I can actually say its part of my story. It's the reason why I am the individual I am today. I have learned so much in my life. I have always lived a life to be grateful because I had my share of struggles. My traumatic experience taught me at a young age to appreciate all that was given to me. My family, my whole world, they fill my heart to its fullest. The beauty in today is outstanding. To breath and listen to the sounds of the birds, the water, the leaves they are all so beautiful. Sounds and images I took for granted for so many years. I am on a mission now, a mission to live life to its fullest. I got caught up on going up the corporate ladder, having the best electronics, the latest fashions or the expensive trips but now I ask myself, why? What truly is most valuable to me right now? I look at my children and they view life so simple, yet I would internalize situations and make them appear much more complicated than what they really were. It was my assumptions, judgments, and fear that made situations seem problematic. My experience forced me to take a halt, to stop and face reality in a way that I could have never prepared myself for, but the journey it took me on was a journey that I will forever be grateful for. A journey that allowed me to see my inner self, the spiritual side that views life in a way that is far more beautiful than what the eye can see. I now cherish life to its fullest, the beauty in everything and everyone that surrounds me. I now can think of my father and be happy for the years that I spent with him versus the years I had without him. All of these experiences are priceless.

Like everyone, I have had obstacles. Obstacles that sometimes questioned everything I believed in. It questioned my faith, it questioned my strength, it questioned my health both physically and mentally. Yet in the end I always survived. That's the key point, "we CAN and will survive!" I have always lived my life with a, "positive thinking" attitude and truthfully I do believe that is exactly what has allowed me to overcome the obstacles or challenges that I have been faced with throughout my life. I went to see a counselor in recent months (to help me deal with what had recently occurred with our family) and as I began to tell my life story, family history etc. I also mentioned that through it all I have always had a willpower (if you want to call it that) to overcome any challenge with a positive attitude; with every challenge that there was a lesson to be learned and to take that knowledge and do something powerful with it. Over the years, I have always been fortunate that my family, my finances, my career have been exactly what I have always wanted and envisioned. I truly believe the power in positive thinking and that at this moment, this too will be a challenge that I will continue to learn and grow.

The counselor literally scratched his head and said, "It's people like you that make us psychiatrists, psychologists, and counselors scratch our heads." How do people like yourself who have been dealt with challenges that you have and yet continue to be successful and with a positive and open mind? My exact response was "positive thinking, that's what you can take back to your professionals." Now, I'm not going to lead you to believe that I have any professional accreditations to indicate that I am a PhD or DR of any sort (because I don't), but I will say that I do believe with every fiber of my being that positive thinking is what helped me get through my challenges. I hope it can do the same for you.

In my opinion, positive thinking is about having faith and believing in you. Taking steps in the direction that leads you to where you want to go. Whether they are baby steps or giant steps, it makes no difference so long as you are taking the steps in the direction to the better you. Sitting at home and dreaming about what you want in life, is wonderful but what are YOU going to do to make it happen. Sitting at home and visualizing, is not the only thing you need to make things change in your life. You need to take action! Whatever that action is, you will know inside. Take the time for yourself to self discover what really makes you happy. What are you passionate about? What do you love more than anything? What truly makes you happy? Take those answers and follow your gut, follow your inner self. It's more powerful, more wonderful than anything you could envision.

I'm still on my journey to making a difference. My goal is to make change in the mental health sector; to give teens and young adults the support and love that they deserve. We can help our youth in providing coping strategies, teach them to inspire, motivate and empower not only themselves but also others. Make them happy and well-rounded individuals. They will be able pass it along to others and continue to do so as they move on with their lives.

I have faith, hope and believe that my words today will lead me to do great things in the future. What that future looks like I don't know, but for the first time in a long time, I don't want to know. I am enjoying the present; the now because that's what life is intended to be. My past is behind, my future is whatever will be, will be and now is a gift. We all are given the gift of one life, I'm living mine to its fullest. Are you?

"A teacher affects eternity and one can never tell where their influence stops"

By Henry Adams

Chapter *16*

Pain

I n January 2017, I enrolled in a couple college courses, mental health and psychology; I wanted to have a better understanding of the effects and the impacts of mental health and a basic understanding how the brain works. My professor, an incredible woman whose dedicated her time to educate others about mental health and the stigma that is connected around it. She helped me understand the reality of mental illness. Her teachings made me realize that individuals, who have mental illnesses or addictions, don't end up that way because that's what they wanted for themselves. My ignorance made me a fool in that aspect. No one wakes up one day and says, I'm going to be an addict or I'm going to feel depressed or look down on myself? No one envisions that for there future; sometimes people are in pain, for one reason or another, people are in pain. At times I felt my pain surrounded me, consumed me and sometimes I felt like I couldn't change a thing. Eventually I made a choice. I wasn't going to allow my pain to lead me down a road I didn't want to travel.

Does it make anyone any less of a person because there pain caused them to make a negative choice to help cope and deal with their own challenges? No, and yet for years I thought yes. For years I struggled trying to understand why individuals couldn't be positive. Couldn't just make the choice to be positive and do positive things in the world. Something that came very natural to me. My professor helped me understand; that it was a choice in coping with pain. Pain, that I too had from my past, but I'm grateful that my choices had been positive. The difference is now I realize, I could have very easily been one of those individuals who chose a negative option. It doesn't make anyone stronger or better that they were fortunate to have chosen the positive path, if anything, we all need to have empathy for those who didn't. It could have very easily been anyone of us. That's what I learned from that class. I learned that so many individuals struggle because of pain, whether it's fear, anger, sadness etc. It's all from pain and coping from that pain can lead to addictions, depression, anxiety, alcohol, shopping and so many other negative options. Once I understood that, my mindset completely changed. I realized that everyone is a gift; every person deserves happiness despite the choices they make in life. Everyone is amazing and unique in their own way.

I will never be the person who I once was, a person that thought making the choice to be positive was so easy. A person that looked differently at those individuals who appeared less than the "norm." Positivity, something I once believed was as easy as brushing teeth, I now know that it's not that easy for everyone. I was one of the fortunate ones who learned at a young age that positivity works. Works beyond belief. If this book and my words, help educate you, help you understand that positivity works and will change your life then I have done what I wanted to do with this book. I want everyone to see life in a positive way; there is no other way to live. What a world this would be, if everyone lived the life of positivity and spread it to everyone and anyone they met.

Chapter *17*

Who I am now

When I began writing my story, the intent was to make a difference in mental health. To improve how people are treated, medication dosage, increase in communication, compassion and empathy. I intend to hopefully do all of those things. Allowing our teens, young adults the opportunity they need for a second chance, a chance to let them know that they will survive this; they will overcome struggles. Everyone deserves to be treated with respect, appreciation and with love. The changes I am hoping to make will give these youth that opportunity. I want to be part of a team that helps empower these incredible individuals to realize and believe that they have an amazing life to live. To teach, inspire, motivate and empower each and every one of them. Help them believe in themselves, the support of others and believe that they can come out of this stronger and better than ever. There are always people who want to help. I want to show life is beautiful just like each and every one of them. They are beautiful inside and out.

Along this journey, this path that had me originally making change for mental health had also taught me so much more. I learned more about myself than ever before. My journey was always to inspire and motivate others, but in my mind I wasn't clear how that was to be? How was I going to make the difference that I felt I had to make? During this journey, it also became about love. Love for myself, my true inner self and love for everyone and everything that surrounded me. Love above all will provide happiness to each and every one of us. The majority of my adult life I spent running around and chasing dreams that I created for myself. I chose a life of always sayings *yes* and never saying *no*. The word, *"no"* was rarely in my vocabulary because for some reason I thought I had to show the world that I could handle anything and everything. There was never a day where I didn't have something planned whether it was my hectic work schedule, kids sports, cleaning etc. The worst is when I didn't have anything planned; I would create something. Someone in my family surely needed my assistance; after all, some of my extended family were aging and they needed me. There I was constantly making plans, the thought of sitting at home and relaxing sounded outrageous to me. Who had time for that?

I found it so strange, how each and every one of my friends always thought my house was immaculate. Clean to the nines, perfect in every way, yet I never thought it was clean enough? How can that be? What did my friends see that I couldn't see? A house that was clean to others still felt cluttered, disorganized or dirty to me. My work life was very much the same. I took pride in working hard and having my leaders; peers and employees know that they could depend on me in every way possible. I felt as though I could never say no despite the work piling that at times consumed me. In my mind, there were times when I knew I couldn't take on another task, I was on overload, but I couldn't say no. It's not in my nature; I didn't want to disappoint them. But who is them? Why wasn't it ever me? Why didn't I always check what I wanted to do, first? This whole experience has now gotten me to realize why I was living the adult life I had.

18

Rollercoaster ride

A t times, I feel I am on a self-discovery rollercoaster. When the ride will end, I don't know but I'm enjoying the ride. When I think of the person I was vs the person I am today I see many similarities and yet just as many differences. Could this life experience have changed me this much? I think so. Am I still a dependable, strong, independent women? Yes. Am I still the social gal that loves spending time with friends and family? Yes. Am I still dedicated and hardworking in everything and anything I apply myself to? Yes. BUT, and that's a big but...something is different now. Something has changed within me, something as beautiful and as breathtaking as a beautiful sunset across any lake or ocean. I was and always will be the positive individual that I am. I will always be grateful for each and every day I have had and have today. Life is a gift; there is no other way to live. Peace, joy, love and happiness all qualities I thought I had and maybe I did but at a completely different scale. The peace, joy, love and happiness that I have today is the peak of the roller coaster. The high that only true happiness can feel, it's magical; it's whimsical in every sense of the word. It's a feeling I didn't know was possible. Some will say this is a mid life crisis or maybe it's my age but I don't believe so. Suddenly realizing that life slips away just as quickly as the summer flashes by makes me see life differently. In any case, this experience has allowed me to become a new and energized me. Previously, I took on everything that came my way, but here I am approaching forty (wow, I can't tell you how quickly that came up!) and now beginning to know who I really am and why I do the things I do. My behaviours, my actions, my responses, it all makes sense now. Prior to this moment I worked hard that at times I felt over tired (both physically and mentally), yet some wouldn't have known it. I tried not to show it, I couldn't. It was all perception, I had to have people: family, friends and coworkers always know that I had it all together not just one hundred percent but one hundred twenty percent of the time. There were never enough hours in a day to get things done but that didn't matter to me, I was getting it done despite the timeframe I created for myself.

That's what I realize now; I created this. I created this image, this mask or masks. I'm beginning to realize I had several masks that I can no longer carry any more, and even more importantly nor do I want to. A work mask, a family mask, a friend mask, each and every one of them were masks, not masks to its fullest, many people new parts of me but none new all of me. I somehow, somewhere created facades that lead me to believe that no one could really know the true me. It's now, that I realize I made that choice, no one made that choice for me it was me. These masks were barriers that I created for myself. Only now am I figuring this out. I made choices to do something, anything that would fill my days. Sitting down and resting was never the option for me. I realize now, I chose this because I couldn't let my mind rest. I didn't want to hear what it had to say. I had pain. Pain that I tried desperately to tuck away. No one could ever know what really happened. I see now that the hectic life style I created for myself was also to protect myself. Protect me from the anger and pain. It was a long time ago that I chose to bury all those hurt feelings and emotions. At the time, it's what I thought was the best solution.

As I went into adulthood, married with children I chose to make myself indescribably busy all the time. Bedtime was even on the go; I rarely had good night sleeps. My mind would go in circles of things that I had to do. Now I realize I never HAD to do anything, I choose to do everything.

Chapter 19

Living for Today

For the first time in a long time, I am truly happy and full of love. My inner self is finally at peace. What's interesting about the whole experience, I didn't realize that any of this was an issue until I was forced to look within. It was through life challenges that were presented which forced me to ask myself, "who really am I?" Today, I read countless books (something I rarely did in the past, I told myself I didn't have time), books that help and continue to give me the guidance to live the life that I am intended to live. No more saying yes to everything, no more filling my days with everything I could think off. No more. Now it's time to enjoy the paths of today. Today, it's ok to have a crumb on the countertop or a piece of dirt on the floor. I finally know that, it's ok. It doesn't make me a terrible person to not have the laundry caught up each and every day, it doesn't make me a terrible person if I'm not the top performer at work, it doesn't make me a terrible person if my kids are late to a sporting event. It just doesn't.

Today is a new day, a new me. A life I now know I was intended to live, a life full of peace, love and harmony. Life doesn't have to be so complicated; I made it that way. I made a choice to fill my days with countless amount of "things I have to do." Did I really though? Today I realize life is not about the things I do or the things I own. It has everything to do with the love I have for myself. Now, I truly feel the love that I can spread to others is limitless. This took time for silence, deep breaths and me. I learned to stop the noise of everything that consumed my life. I made it a habit to have noise all day and every day, whether it was a "to do list", work, chores etc. Silence was never an option. Silence.... quiet.... truly hearing my inner self. It's such a beautiful thing, such an incredible feeling. I live with true eternal love, a feeling that only those who have already experienced will understand and comprehend. A feeling I wish every human could and should have. Something remains different but in a good way, something changed that I haven't put my exact finger on. Perhaps it's the quietness that I have allowed in my life or maybe it's the lesson that I now learned living in the NOW is far more enjoyable than ever living in the past or future. Maybe, it's that I'm just enjoying life. I was accustomed to the hectic days, the running around, the fun times with friends and suddenly it's not a must for me, suddenly the nature walks, the sounds of birds, the sounds of the waves, the beauty and the stillness of our world is far more enjoyable than anything else. My family and friends are a very special part of my life, a life that I now truly can enjoy to its fullest. In this transformation, now I can just be. I can finally just be here and now. Enjoy every moment of now and what it has to offer. No more worrying about how others perceived me, how do I perceive myself? That's the question I avoided to ask myself until now. No more planning for the future and making sure that everything I had set out to do at a given time frame was achieved. No more. No more judging others for their behaviours and life choices. Who am I to judge?

I don't know when my concerns about how others perceived me weighed heavily that I would do anything for people's acceptance. I don't know when I began to cast judgment on those individuals who didn't "succeed" in life. All of these things, all of my actions suddenly all make sense to me. I needed more, but didn't know I needed it. I have found a new love in today, a new love in me, a new love in my surroundings. There is not one day now that I don't give thanks to God for what I have been given and what I continue to receive.

I am very fortunate to have a husband such as my mine who agreed to allow me the time that I needed to truly figure out who I wanted to be, where I want to go with the second part of my life. I decided I was going to give myself one year, one year off work, being with my family and understanding me. Initially, I wasn't sure what my true calling was. I needed to take more time and understand who I am and why I am that person today. I understand that my true calling is perhaps to do what I am doing now. To write, to write about my deepest thoughts, thoughts I once held so tight that it took a deadbolt to open. Now it's time, it's time to express my deepest thoughts in hopes that I can share and help others. Give guidance where someone may not have known they needed it. Give faith to those who maybe didn't know where to turn to. Give hope to those who feel there is no hope in sight.

Faith, Hope, Believe. Three powerful words I have hung onto tightly the last year, three words that I cherished and read daily. I had to have faith in myself, understand who I really was. Who are you? Who do you want the world to see? I know it's someone incredible. I never gave up on hope. Don't give up on hope; hope is powerful. I had hope in my family, friends, aspirations, love, success, health, happiness and much more. I had hope and believed in all the things I wanted in life. Without hope, I knew life could feel empty. I had to stop it from happening. Do you have hope? Do you tell yourself that you are beautiful? Do you tell yourself you are talented? Do you tell yourself you are incredible (because you are)? If you can't, please ask for help. Professionals are here to help you feel beautiful again.

Sometimes I questioned everything I believed in, my God, myself, my family, my friends, my career, I questioned everything. But there came a time when I realized I had to return to my belief in faith and hope. I had to believe in everything I was given, I believed that everything and everyone surrounding me was and is for a purpose. With that, I believed in the universe and everything that life had to offer. I believed that I could make a difference with the challenges I had been faced with. I believed that God, the universe or my high self would guide me when I had to change direction or continue on the same path. I believed and still do today.

I am unbelievably grateful for the people that surround me each and everyday. My family and friends mean the world to me, I pray that each of them have an abundance of love, health and happiness. The difference now is, my love, health and happiness also mean the world to me too. It's truly a beautiful gift, to understand and appreciate the inner peace, love and joy that every single one of us has inside of us. The trouble is, how far down inside is it? That's a question you need to ask yourself. If it's buried, bring it to the forefront. The deep inner peace is something that everyone deserves to live with. I now know that buried behind my smiles, my eagerness to say yes and take on everything, my need to please others was a whole lot of sadness, anger, and shame. Once I rediscover myself, allowed myself the quiet time, the silence my mind and body craved and needed, I reached inner peace and inner love. I can say with utmost certainty it was well worth the travel, a travel that was emotional, long and hard, but certainly worth it. I know now that my body craved this inner peace almost, if not just as much as food and water. We all want to have peace, love and happiness. Love was right in front of my face, my family, my closest friends and yet at times I allowed my day-to-day stressors take me away from the those who made me truly happy. If you feel alone, please search for a support group or some additional services and/or programs that can help you. There are people out there who care about your well-being. Allow yourself to feel whatever feelings that need to be felt. It's meant to be that way. Allow yourself to cry for the situations that deserve the tears you shed. Allow yourself to be happy for the memories and the joys that you have had and have today. I allowed myself to feel, the feelings that needed to be felt and acknowledged. The important part was I moved forward, moved past those emotions and moved to the joy, peace and love that I yearned for. It's in all of us and each and every one of us deserves it.

I also had to forgive. Forgive those who hurt me or who I hurt. I knew I had to forgive not for those around me, but for myself and for my well-being. Do you need to forgive yourself and/or forgive someone who hurt you? It was during my focus on forgiveness that allowed me to move forward, move past from the anger. Allowing myself to forgive, finally it allowed me to breath.

Chapter 20

The Windows

The old me kept the windows shut so the dust didn't come in, the old me put the outdoor cushions away daily so the colour didn't fade, the old me never went outside without a purpose. The new me, the new me leaves the windows open every chance I get to welcome the rain, the sunshine, the sounds of nature. The new me leaves the cushions out all summer long because I want them to be welcoming to myself, my friends and family for the memories and conversations we continue to make and the new me is outside every moment I have, but this time, without a purpose. No purpose to keep the lawn perfect, no purpose to keep every single weed out, no purpose but to sit and enjoy the beauty of today, the beauty that surrounds family, my friends and me. That's the new me.

"Like a river flows
Surely to the sea
Darling, so it goes
Some things are meant to be
Take my hand,
Take my whole life, too,
For I can't help falling in love with you"

-Elvis Presley (song: Can't Help Falling in Love)

Chapter 21

Can't Help Falling In Love

M y husband and I were out last night, enjoyed a fun filled evening with dinner and dancing. We sat by the beach afterwards; our city is fortunate to be surrounded by beautiful beaches. We looked at the waves crashing; we listened to the sounds of the waves, and inhaled the beautiful evening crisp air. We sat and enjoyed each other's company, something we rarely do, something we should make more of an effort to do and still we don't. We spoke of the beauty of living in the now, the inner gratification, the inner peace, love and enjoyment we have when we live in the now. Last night, "Can't Help Falling In Love" by Elvis Presley came on, a song that my father loved, a song that I have never been able to hear since his passing. Elvis was his idol. A song that would force me to run out of the building, run and hide before tears would shed. Yes, that's what that song did to me each every time it played for the past twenty-seven years. Last night, it was different. My husband and I were already dancing prior to the song and he instantly asked if I wanted to go, he knew all too well what this song did to me. But something was different, something inside me told me to stay and dance with my husband who I love so much and dance to this beautiful song. Emotions were high as the memories flashed back when my father used to sing this song to my mother. The lyrics were as beautiful as I remembered them. For the first time, I didn't cry, I didn't run away, I faced it. I faced the song, the song that was a symbol of my past that I chose to bury so long ago. Last night, was the night that I danced with my husband to the song that my father loved so much. Last night, truly was the beginning for me. I know that I have moved on, moved forward from the pain that I had, but did not recognize for so long. The pain from my father's death. I can now really take my husband's hand, take "my whole life too, and keep falling in love with you."

"*Life is 10% of what happens and 90% is how you react to it.*"

Charles R. Swindoll

Chapter 22

Twelve Years

It truly is interesting how life has these signs that are telling us that the universe, God, our higher self is listening, watching and guiding us.

Last night, my husband, two wonderful friends and myself went to a charity event to support our community and our local Hospital to raise funds for mental health.

During this event, this event intended for mental health, a cause that now holds near and dear to my heart. Our friends and I were enjoying the evening, the drinks, the laughter, and the music. As we stood and listened to a band who had been playing a mixture of songs varying from rock to country, who would have guessed that this band, a band I have never heard of before, would end up playing a church song in the middle of their mix of music. We thought it was strange, a little odd, but went with it. Within seconds it was very clear to my husband and I what song was being played. The church song that for years made me cry, a song that I could not run from like the one from Elvis, a song that I forced myself to listen to in church simply because I didn't want to cause a scene during mass. A song, that made my eyes well up and my body numb each and every time I heard it. The song was, "Hallelujah." It was played at my father's funeral. Another connection, another link to my past, my father and the funeral I chose to block from my memory so long ago. Now, I stood before a rock band, at a local mental health charity event and the song, the song from church is being played. My friends had somehow mysteriously disappeared so my husband and I stood alone. He looked at me and I looked at him, each of us knowing what the other was thinking. This is a sign, he says to me. There is no coincidence here. Our thoughts were connected.

Here is my recap, two evenings back to back, two songs, two defining songs of my past, both played. Two songs that were the definition of pain and heartache for me, that given a time frame I heard no more than two or three times a year, now being played before my husband and I in only a matter of hours from one another.

Many would say this is coincidence, some would say, that's a fluke, I choose to believe it was far more special than that. Both songs played, both songs I listened without one tear, without numb, without the fear that the pain will all come rushing back. I am finally at peace and able to listen and enjoy both songs, to sing the songs that once caused me pain, to dance and create new memories and delete the pain from yesterday. I can now cherish these songs, listen and enjoy the moments I had with my father, enjoy the wonderful twelve years I had with him. Twelve years, not long enough, but now I am able to remember and speak of the joy that I had for those special years. I was the definition of daddy's little girl. I loved him more then anything. He was my everything. I thought he chose to leave me and for years I did not know why. Now I know, you didn't chose to leave me, now I know you were hurting. Now I know you too were in pain. I love you daddy. Maybe you gave me signs here on earth for several years, maybe I chose to ignore them, or maybe you chose not do anything besides watch over my family and me. I believe wholeheartedly those two songs were a sign from you. I'm free of all pain. I love you, rest in peace.

"It's the heart afraid of breaking
That never learns to dance
It's the dream afraid of waking that never
Takes the chance
It's the one who won't be taken
Who cannot seem to forgive
And the soul afraid of dying that never
Learns to live"

Lyrics from The Rose by Westlife

"If I have the belief that I can do it, I shall surely acquire the capacity to do it even if I may not have it at the beginning." Mohandas Karachand Gandhi

Chapter *23*

I can

As I read the book, "I Can Clearly See Now" by Dr Wayne W Dyer. A book I was compelled to borrow from the library, it was a book I knew I had to read. The two simple words in the title that I live as a philosophy perhaps was the reasoning behind it. "I Can," I Can Attitude, two words I live by, two words that have been ingrained in my brain, two words that have made me believe that I can overcome any challenge, any change that happens.

I can do this, I can overcome, I can, I can, I can. This book was so insightful. Dr. Wayne Dyer talks about his life, an incredible one at that, but the most powerful part of it was when he was talking about self-actualization and God-realization. Terminology I knew very little about until recently; however, now finding a strong connection to it all. Here I am now, thirty-nine, reading a book regarding a subject I wanted to explore further. Could it be that the life I lead, the life I have lead actually had a title for it? I had taught myself during my mid teens that nothing was going to change my mindset, that the goals I had set out for myself would happen because I was going to make sure they happened. Somehow as a teen I believed that my past experiences made people assume that I was going to make poor life choices and not amount to anything. Did I make poor choices? Absolutely. Did I learn and grow from them? Without a doubt. I had myself believe there were statistics that showed I wasn't going to be successful based on my life experiences. Was there ever any statistics? I think back now and realize there never was. I never read it, no one ever told me that, yet, somehow I told myself that. However, it was those statistics, past studies that made me overcome my challenges. At a young age I felt as though I needed to prove that I was not going to become a statistic. I CAN and was going to be successful. An attitude I adapted in my late teens and continue to do so today.

I have lived a life where I have always set goals for myself; it's the way I choose to live. Each goal I fixated on it until I achieved it. It's the drive inside, the determination inside that kept me going. It allowed me to believe that I would reach my goals. Each time that it happened, when I hit my target, I took note, noticed the connection. Appreciating the value in, "mental imaging" believing with my whole heart that things will turn out the way I believe them to be. I don't know when I learned this. It came at a young age, before I even hit my teens. Somehow, this came natural to me.

Here I was now, reading a fascinating book by an incredible author and became informed that the life I lead had studies behind it. Well-educated people, believed in what I have felt and feel so strongly about.

My education in the past has always been business related courses. Focusing on the goal of working at a bank, it only made sense. A goal I set for myself at a young age of seven or eight. My education in psychology, how the brain works or behaviours is courses I chose to ignore. At the time, it wasn't in my mindset; the financial industry was my focus, my goal, my vision.

Now, thirty-nine taking a different road, finding behaviours, the brain, psychology all intriguing but also recognizing that my way of thinking has many related behaviours like those that I'm reading or studying. Self-actualization, a life I lead. To believe, to teach and show others that the life that you want to lead does happen, can happen. You just have to believe in it, believe in yourself. This book, like many that involved spiritual and positive thinking only took me days to read. I enjoyed it very much, I could relate to the words I was reading. I hope that by sharing my story someone else can believe it themself to. Life has choices everyday; everywhere you turn there are choices, a choice either negative or positive. A choice that can lead to great, wonderful circumstances but also can lead to sad, horrible circumstances. Why choose sad and horrible? Why choose negative rather than the alternative? Life is believing in yourself, positive thoughts, positive choices, positive images. Life is a choice in the life you want to live. Stay true to what makes you feel good inside, makes you feel love inside, the life that everyone deserves to live. Choose positive, choose self-actualization.

"When you let the ANTs (automatic negative thoughts) become undisciplined, they infest your mind, and become the seeds for anxiety and depression." - Dr Daniel Amen

"the Blame Game undermines your sense of personal power. That is why it is most poisonous ANT of all." - Dr Daniel Amen

Chapter 24

Ants

This past year I have done more reading then I have in the past thirty-nine years of my life. I have found it fascinating, the information I have learned. Most recent, I read a book by Dr. Daniel Amen "Unleash the power of the female brain." Incredible book, I enjoyed it very much. There were many takeaways but one stood out to me. ANTS, pesky little ANTS. He describes our negative thoughts as ANTs (automatic negative thoughts). What a perfect way to describe our negative thoughts. Pesky ants.

All of these worries, stressed, and anxiety I caused myself solely because my assumptions and judgments. No one around me told me to feel this way, yet sometimes they would consume me. Most of my negative thoughts were my own assumptions.

I always internalized how people felt about me, if I upset someone, if someone misunderstood, etc. These thoughts caused stress and anxiety.

I have now learned to turn those thoughts into positive. Flip them upside down, if you will.

Why did I internalize everything? Why did I blame others for my life experiences? Why couldn't I just accept the way things as they were?

I have learned thru my experiences, thru reading and my own personal beliefs that my, "ANTs" hurt me more than anyone else. So why do so many people choose to live that way? Have I lived the "perfect" life, absolutely not. What is the perfect life? My greatest challenges in life proved to show my greatest strengths. When we make mistakes, we want to be forgiven; and yet some people choose not to forgive others. Once I accepted my past, the blaming I clung onto suddenly became a puff of smoke. Blaming someone for my life experiences only intensified a life with negativity. I chose to forgive and let go.

People do the best that they can with what they have. Sometimes, it's less than ideal there's no denying that, but still it was the best they could do.

You or I cannot assume the pain, suffering or negative thoughts that were inflicted on others that were part of their family. Blaming, assuming and never letting go affects more ourselves than anyone else around you.

You are the only one that can make the choice to love *yourself* and others.

You are the only one that can choose to let go and forgive. Let go of those negative feelings/thoughts.

You are the only one that can choose to stop making assumptions of others around you.

Stay true to yourself, stay true to the best you. It's inside you. Sometimes it gets buried with life experiences and pressures but trust me it CAN resurface.

Believe in yourself and let go of the negative.

"All of my people need love, I give some
'Cause in the end, the love we take's
Got nothing on the love we make
So give love
So give love
So give love"

Give love by Andy Grammer

Chapter

25

Give love

Many of us get caught up in our own day-to-day stresses and forget to "check ourselves." Often life is hectic with struggles, and pressures that our behaviours can be less than appealing to the outside world. It's important how we treat others despite the type of day or days we are having.

Often my stress would be passed onto others who have no relevance at all to the situation, yet somehow I found it acceptable to take it out on them. Kindness and love to others, is something that is rewarding all in itself, and yet at times when I wasn't at my best it is the one thing that I would lose sight of. Why did I succumb to giving up on the one thing that could instantly give joy not only to me, but also to others? Love and kindness are truly the world's best medicine; something that each and every one of us should live a daily life full of.

Take for example; my son and I were at Starbucks. Patiently waiting for our turn. In front of us stood a woman with, what seemed to be, her teenage daughter. There was only one cashier, a beautiful young lady doing her best, taking orders, collecting cash and making the beverages. This young lady was taking and filing the orders, likely making minimum wage, trying to move quickly as a line was forming.

The lady in front of me, with extreme attitude gave this young lady the most horrible treatment. The customer's drink was not prepared to level of standards that she expected. It was very clear by her facial expression, and her body language that she was not satisfied. The beverage had spilt over the rim and onto the outside of the cup. The customer cleaned her cup with a bunch of napkins, tossed the lid and napkins, and told the cashier to clean the mess since this was obviously her fault. What gives someone the right to treat someone with such disrespect?

I was appalled that someone could treat another human being with such little respect for something so minor. I'm not ignorant to believe that unfortunately this happens more often than I could imagine, BUT why do we allow ourselves to behave this way and tell ourselves it's ok? It's NOT ok. It's never ok to treat someone with disrespect.

I quickly stuck up for the cashier, told the customer, the cashier is doing the best that she can, given the resources that she had (which was none). I told the cashier not to worry about the mess the customer created I would clean it up.

I asked the cashier, to take a deep breath and take her time in making my beverages.

My sons, God bless him, said to me after we walked away.... "Mom, did you just give that lady a life lesson?" I smiled and said, "Yes son, I guess I did."

I hope that customer thought twice about how she treated the rest of the people she interacted with for the rest of that day. If each one of us can stand up for one other, respect one another, and support one another our world, our lives would be nothing less than extraordinary.

We need to respect one another, help one another and most importantly love one another. We have it in us; we have the ability to make a difference for the greater good for our community and mankind.

If you find yourself stressed, irritated or "short fussed " as some would say, take a few moments. Take a few breaths and "check yourself". Take a moment and check the behaviour you are exhorting to others. I am much aware of myself now.

Am I showing love and kindness OR hate, bitter and rudeness? I catch myself saying, "check myself." To ensure I am treating others with the respect, kindness, and love that everyone deserves. Is this who I really want to be?

PART 3

My Strategies

My life strategies on how I changed my worst moments:

1. Be grateful
2. Stay Positive
3. Daily acts of kindness
4. Live in the now - Self Help Books and/or videos
5. Meditation, Yoga, Prayer
6. Vision Board
7. Interaction with friends and friend. Surround yourself with love
8. Exercise
9. Positive Music/TV
10. Forget the past, let it become your story
11. Nature walks - Listen to yourself
12. Educate yourself
13. Inspirational quotes
14. Fill yourself with love- stop judgements and assumptions (it's only your perception)
15. Unplug from social media, find a healthy balance
16. Life isn't a schedule
17. Pets, they are therapeutic
18. Seek professional help
19. Forgiveness

"When you arise in the morning, give thanks for the morning light, for your life and strength. Give thanks for your food and the joy of living. If you see no reason for giving thanks, the fault lies with yourself."

-By Tecumseh, Shawnee Native American Leader.
The Magic Book by Rhonda Byrne

Chapter

1

Be Grateful

B e grateful. Those words were easy to read, to type or to even to say as opposed to actually feeling grateful at certain times in my life. The days when I questioned everything had the pity party or the days when I wouldn't leave my home; those were the days that I made a priority to sit and think about what I was grateful for. There was always going to situations, challenges, losses, pain that would hold me back from seeing and realizing all the wonderful things that I had to be thankful for. It's those experiences that forced me to remember how fortunate I actually was. Grateful for what I had at that present moment.

I wrote a gratitude list on my low days. Whether it was one or ten, it didn't matter. I read them, daily. Some days, those grateful pointers I wrote only days ago would literally mean nothing to me days later. Some days I felt no emotion, no feeling towards those sentences I felt so strongly about only day's prior. But as I continued to add and read those wonderful and thankful positive attributes daily, my positive feelings came back to me. I felt the gratitude in my heart again. I was thankful, grateful for everything I still had in my life. I reflected on what truly made me happy. Was it my job, money, house, or people? It was the values and beliefs of the job, it was the experiences I created with the money I earned, it was the memories made in my home and it was the connections and the relationships I had with people. There was always something to be grateful for despite whatever was happening in my life. I just had to look deep inside me at times. Life itself is something to be grateful for.

Each morning I wake up, I look out my window and I say thank you for another day. Thank you for my health, both mentally and physically. Thank you for my family and friends, thank you for the food and day that lies ahead because I know it's going to be great. More importantly thank you for filling me with love.

It reminds me to appreciate the simple things in life. I encourage you to give it a try, even if it's only for one or two weeks. Try it; see if you feel any different, what do you have to lose? You are a strong and determined individual who will see the brighter days ahead.

"Nobody can go back and start a new beginning, but anyone can start today and make a new ending."

-By Maria Robinson

Chapter   *2*

Stay Positive

S tay positive. I have stayed true to that statement my entire adult life. I have always made a conscious decision to see things in a positive way. It's a choice that I chose to make. Glass half empty, glass half full. Why make the choice to see the glass as half empty? I started by just that, looking at a glass as half full. l noticed I felt better inside when I looked at things in a more positive way. Positive thinking has been very powerful in my life, it's a choice I have always believed in and strongly and am passionate about. It has made a difference in every situation that I am faced with both positive and negative. I am much more self-aware now and realize quickly when I am being negative. I am the only one that ultimately can make the change in how I see my life experiences. It's easy to blame others, have the pity party and always have the, "why me?" I allowed myself the time I needed to cry, to have the low days, the pity party, they were all ok BUT I gave myself a choice, a timeframe when I had to make the switch. Make the switch to do something positive with what I learned and/or discovered. I believed by making the choice of being positive, I was going to lead a life of love, health and happiness. Staying positive changed my life, but I knew staying negative could have also done the same (in a far less than desirable way). I made a choice, made a choice everyday when I woke up. Be positive, stay positive and give thanks to everything and everyone that surrounds me.

"Be kind, for everyone you meet is fighting a hard battle."

-By Philo of Alexandria (CIRCA 20 BC-AD 50) Philosopher

Chapter

3

Daily Acts Of Kindness

Daily acts of kindness. Being kind to others, there is never anything negative you can take away from that. Kindness is about showing love to others, treated others with respect and dignity. Acts of kindness have the ability to brighten people's lives. In my mind, kindness is contagious. When I see someone do an act of kindness, I feel this sudden urge to follow suit. Something as simple as a stranger who pays for my Tim Horton's coffee in the drive-thru line, I immediately have this urge to do something good. Has that happened to you? Can you relate? There are so many people out in the world who care for the well being of others, the kindness that everyone deserves. It truly is remarkable; this world is filled with so many amazing people. People who want to make a difference not only for themselves but also for others.

I remember the day I saw, "Kindness Diaries" on Netflix. It was one of those days where I needed a little something to brighten my day, and boy did that do it. The short thirteen episode series was about an individual by the name of Leon Logothetis who made an incredible decision to quit his job and travel the world with no money or food, but just his motorbike. The intent was for him to see if he could travel the world based on people's kindness by offering him a place to stay, food, gas etc. I'm not about to tell you the ending to this wonderful series; however, to me it was so inspirational. I watched the series in less than a day and half, but I was excited and fascinated by what he was learning and what he was showing the world. This series inspired me to do the same thing, but on a much smaller scale. I programmed a daily task reminder on my phone— Daily Act of Kindness.

I was at the grocery store waiting to checkout. In the past, I was usually checking emails, texting, viewing social media or planning for the days and weeks ahead in my mind. Living in the now has changed that for me. In front of me was a woman with a baby packing her groceries. It was very clear that she wasn't having the best day. It was evident she was trying to keep herself composed and hold back tears. I likely would not have noticed this in my past previous habits of checking emails etc. When it was my turn, the cashier apologized to me, "I'm sorry, I'm just thinking about my last customer." It was clear the poor woman ahead of me had impacted her as well. I was surprised to find the distraught lady parked right in front me, unloading her groceries. I felt this overwhelming need to help her, but I didn't know how. I looked in my car, I looked in my wallet and although I didn't have much to give, I had ten dollars. I went up to her and said, "I know you don't know me but I noticed in the grocery store you weren't having a great day. Here's ten dollars take it and go for an ice cream with your child or do something that can brighten your day just a little bit." As she, teared with gratitude, we exchanged hugs and words of "God bless you." I can't tell you how much that impacted me for the rest of the day and days to come. It made me feel stronger, made me feel powerful, made me feel energized and I'm hoping that lady (I never got her name) also had a sense of strength, power and energy. I'm not saying kindness always involves money; there are so many ways we can show kindness by our actions. Volunteering, helping an individual cross a street, unload groceries etc. These acts of kindness can change how the rest of your day goes, a day for the better.

Our family dinners used to consist of communicating the best part and the lowest part of our day. I recently changed that. We now talk about two highs of our day, one thing we are grateful for, or one act of kindness that we completed. It's unbelievable the shift in conversation when changing the topic to something so much more positive. We fixated our conversations on the "low" of our day and now we talk about the "act of kindness" that someone had completed that day. It's an incredible feeling, especially after leaving the dinner table.

Incorporating a daily act of kindness into my day has made an impact on my life and hopefully others as well.

"Nothing you face will be too much for you. You will overcome every obstacle, outlast every challenge, and come through every difficulty better off than you were before."

- By Joel Osteen

Chapter

4

Live in the Now

It took something devastating to force me to change my ways. It took a mixture of emotions for weeks and months before I reached the point of enjoying the true meaning of living in the now. For me, self-help books definitely helped me get there. The first inspirational book that I read was, The Secret by Rhonda Byrne. An amazing co-worker of mine let me borrow it. It was then that I realized that I had been living a life similar to 'The Secret.' This uplifting, motivating and inspirational book, re-confirmed the power in believing in my visions. It motivated me to continue on the unknown path that I was on. I have read many inspirational books since then, each and every one of them profound in their own way. Quotes that I have found interesting or thought provoking I have included in this book, I hope you find them equally inspiring as I have.

Another book I enjoyed was Embracing Uncertainty by Susan Jeffers. There was a specific prayer that Susan included in her book that I find worth repeating.

"Dear God, I trust that no matter what happens in my life, it is for my highest good. And no matter what happens in the

lives of those I love, it is for the highest good. From all things you put before us, we shall become stronger and more loving people. I am grateful for all the beauty and opportunity you put into my life. And in all that I do, I shall seek to be a channel for your love."

This prayer was powerful to me, gave me strength, and brought me back to my faith. My faith at times that had me questioning, "Is there even a God?" "Why are you doing this to us?" But it was my faith that gave me a sense of hope. Hope that I needed to believe life was going to get better.

Living in the now, is about seeing the beauty that is right in front of us at each present moment. Have you ever experienced that? I make sure that I take a moment of every day to step outside and just be. I listen to the sounds, see the views, smell the scents, and touch the ground. I use all of my senses, take a deep breath, and pay attention to the beauty I have right in front of me. Once I chose to live the life in the now, life became so much simpler. I didn't need all the "things" that I once craved, that I thought were "things" that I needed because that's all that they are, "things." Clothing, makeup, shoes, house ware, furniture, electronics what do they all mean? Do they define who we are as individuals? No they shouldn't, yet our society says it does. I was one of them, one who believed that the "things" I had showed the world who I was. I now know there's no truth in any of it. Living in the now, allows me to live life simply. My closet has less clothes, my house isn't always filled with the latest electronics and my furniture is perfect the way it is because at the end of the day, what does it mean anyways? It means nothing. My house, my car, my vacations, are wonderful, but they mean nothing if I didn't have my family and friends. It is them that make my house a home and my trips a vacation. It's the people in my life that makes me appreciate everything. I can't say that in my twenties and thirties I felt this way, but as I'm nearing my forties I can definitely tell you that I will no longer live life any other way. Living in the now, makes me stop and smell the roses, look at sunsets and clouds, listen to birds chirping and watch the waves crashing on the shore. Allows me to take time and hold hands with my family and friends and just enjoy life. Enjoy life for what it is today. It is truly a beautiful thing.

"I'm proud of who I am
No more monsters, I can breathe again
And you said that I was done
Well, you were wrong and now the best is yet to come
'Cause I can make it on my own
And I don't need you, I found a strength I've never known"

Lyrics from Song "Praying"
- By Kesha

Chapter 5

Meditation, Yoga And Prayer

Meditation, yoga and prayer are three strategies that have played a significant role in my life this past year. I must admit, prior to this, meditation sounded a bit hokey to me, but I can honestly say I was wrong. Meditation is truly uplifting in its own way. When practicing meditation correctly, I truly feel completely relaxed. This exercise has cleared your mind, body and soul. The mornings before I get out of bed and the evenings before I fall asleep, I practice meditation and prayer. From fifteen to thirty minutes I self reflect, letting my mind clear its thoughts of things that I have no use for. It allows me to refresh myself for the day ahead, and get the restful sleep for end of day.

Meditation, yoga and prayer have made an incredible difference in my daily life. It has not only taught me to step away from situations that are less than ideal, but it also has allowed me the opportunity to reflect on myself and reactions that I can avoid. It allows me the time I need to become one with the true me and to appreciate and value what lies deep within. It allows me to appreciate the quiet and let the world carry on as it always does while I become reinvigorated and relaxed. I mediate, practice yoga and pray each day. It's a mindset that has greatly changed my outlook on my everyday activities and stressors. There were days when I felt like life was taking me to down a road where I couldn't handle what was happening. Days that I believed life were teaching me lessons. Those days I often asked, "why me?" Days when I felt like life was escaping before my very eyes. Those were the days, I mediated and prayed so I could relax and calm my mind, body and soul. You and I are beautiful people inside and out. Life has a way to sometimes take the best of ourselves and run wild with it. I allowed myself the quiet, the connection between my body and mind to become one. Meditation, yoga and prayer have done all of those things for me and much more. It has allowed me to see this new profound stillness and beauty within me that I didn't know was there. It re-energizes me, it re-focuses me and re-excites me each and every time I allow myself a simple fifteen minutes.

"Holding on to anger is like grasping a hot coal with the intent of throwing it at someone else; you are the one who gets burned."

- By Gautama Buddha (CIRCA 563 BC - 483 BC) founder of Buddhism

Chapter

6

Vision Board

Some of you might find the vision board a little silly, a little child's play or a little ridiculous but I beg to differ. A vision board was something I used to keep me on track with what I wanted to achieve in life. I created a board of all the things I wanted from family, friends, career, wealth and whatever else I held sacred. I held those visuals somewhere where I could see them each and every day. My vision board consisted of all of my hopes and dreams. It didn't matter if I felt they were unattainable. It didn't matter if I felt I was asking the impossible. It didn't matter if it seemed irrational. My vision board was a way to keep asking myself, What do I really want? What really makes me happy? The vision board gave me hope to what my reality could be. I looked at it and envisioned that the images were already mine. It didn't take long before I began to see things in my life shifting, moving towards what my vision board consisted of. I will tell you right now, although much hasn't come to realization, my life is certainly going into the direction of my vision board, the puzzle of my life. I can't wait until I can see it finished.

"Believe in yourself and all that you are. Know that there is something inside you that is greater than any obstacle."

-By Christian D. Larson

Chapter 7

Socialize With Friends/Family

Many of the words in this book, my emotions, I have kept to myself. In challenging times, difficult times in which I questioned everything, I would rely on my family and friends for support, but then there would be days that I felt I couldn't. At times I felt as though I was completely alone, isolated, that no one understood what I was going through. I think back, and although I had many amazing, wonderful people to lean on, I often chose to isolate myself. It's certainly something I regret. I now look back and wonder why I chose to push my friends and family away times I knew that I needed them. Several reasons come to mind when I think back: shame, embarrassment, everyone is busy, or tired of hearing about my troubles. These were some of the ideas that I told myself. I was wrong for thinking that way. I was fortunate to have family and friends that knew when I needed a lifeline, when I need someone to help me back up. Days when I felt desperate, when I didn't feel like I could crawl out of bed; it was the support of friends that helped me get through it. Days when my support system would knock on my door before I could admit that I needed it. I count my blessings every day for the friends and family I have, the people that have supported my family and me. I will forever be grateful for the people I have in my life, my friends, my companions, and my lifelines. Thank you.

"The greatest glory in living lies not in never falling, but in rising every time we fall."

-By Nelson Mandela

"Do not judge me by my successes, judge me by how many times I fell down and got back up again."

-By Nelson Mandela

Chapter

8

Exercise

E xercise. Not only did it help my physical health, it most definitely helped my mental health, as well. Today exercise continues to be a very important part of my daily life. It helps me feel rejuvenated and uplifted, but above all it helps me stay focused on healthy living. I look back on those challenging days and realize exercise played a huge factor on my mental health and guided me back to the individual I once was and the individual I am today. Exercise whether it's fifteen minutes or one hour daily is so important. Enjoying a walk, run or a bike ride provides me the opportunity to become one with nature, get my exercise and have the quiet time that my mind, body and spirit needs.

I am dedicated to continue my exercise program because I now believe and know that exercise is far from only helping me physically but more importantly mentally as well.

"Be Kind to One Another"

-By Ellen DeGeneres

Chapter

9

Positive Music/TV

P ositive music changed my mood on days that I needed it the most. Many wonderful music artists, who deliver songs with amazing messages, surround us. I have had songs that made me feel numb inside or tears of joy and/or hope just by listening to the lyrics. I have included some lyrics to songs in this book, songs that I have found inspiring and motivating. Whether it's listening to the lyrics or just my commitment to get up and dance foolishly in my home and sing like I am the rock star of singers (which I am in no way shape or form either of the two) music can empower me, motivate me. Music has changed my mood simply by just getting up and dancing. I remember those days during the teen years, when I had a break up or was just feeling low and all I ever did was listen to ballads, listen to music that purposely made me feel even sadder. It was as though I needed confirmation that I should feel this way and I chose to confirm those feelings by picking the saddest songs out there. Why did I do that? I think many of us have done and still do that, but why? Just like life choices, we have a choice in music. Today I pick the music that will inspire and motivate me to carry me throughout my day in the most positive way possible. I pick the music that will empower me to be the best me. I make a conscious choice to be happy, to dance the day away and be grateful that I am blessed with many wonderful musical artists that can provide such an easy therapy. Music is truly an amazing option!

Television shows, there are many to chose from. For me, I gravitate to TV shows and/or movies that make me laugh. Laughter is truly the best medicine. Whether it's TV, computer, laptop, cell phones we can tune into music/tv in just seconds. My go to show is by far Ellen DeGeneres; I can't believe how much one person can truly change your mood in one hour. Somehow, she managed to do that for me in my darkest days. There were days that I struggled a lot, there were days where I didn't want any contact with anyone, but those days I would still dedicate one hour to Ellen. She managed to get me off the couch to dance, even if that dancing was only two, three or four minutes she encouraged me to dance. She always made me laugh. There were some days that laughter seemed so foreign to me, seemed impossible, but it was that one hour with Ellen that I was blessed to experience the joy that she gave not only to her guest but to all of her viewers.

When you make a choice to listen to music, watch a movie, watch TV, and check how you are feeling. Understand your true inner self and decide, what do I need today? Do I need a little laughter? Do I need a little more joy today? Do I need some exercise? If you answer yes to any of these, than choose options like positive music (there are countless out there, YouTube is a wonderful thing), positive movies and/or TV (In my opinion, Ellen is always a guarantee to be a sure thing.)

Some day somebody's gonna make you want to
Turn around and say goodbye
Until then baby are you going to let them
Hold you down and make you cry
Don't you know?
Don't you know things can change
Things'll go your way
If you hold on for one more day

-Lyrics from "Hold On" by Wilson Phillips

Chapter 10

Forget the past; let it become your story

I tried to avoid and block out my past. Yes, we all have a past. I became a perfectionist; a workaholic in all aspects of my life. It took me twenty-seven years and a whole lot of challenges in between to get me to where I am today. I finally had to deal with the challenges that life gave me. I had to accept what was and move forward. I needed time, but then my life changed drastically. Today, I acknowledge my past, but understand that it is more important to move forward. I found the reality of the past too painful to deal with for a long time, but it's funny how the reality finds a way of forcing us to deal with the past of yesterday. When I acknowledged, accepted and moved on from my past, I was able to become a happier person inside and out. The truth is it wasn't my fault, and he did love me. I am proud of the life I have created for myself. My past is finally my past and I can now fully enjoy my present and future with a wonderful and open clear mind.

"Obstacles don't have to stop you,
If you run into a wall,
Don't turn around and give up,
Figure out how to climb it,
Go through it, or work around it."

-By Michael Jordan

Chapter *11*

Nature walks - Listen to you

Nature walks; I wasn't much of a "nature" person. It seemed to me there was always something else that I needed to do. My daily activities, my mind they were always "on the go."

Today, I notice the beauty in nature and the stillness of watching the world around me. I have been blessed with the opportunity to allow myself the time I need for nature walks and listen to what my true inner self wants and needs. It's an amazing gift. When I go out in nature and let my thoughts wonder, I listen to what I have to say. I believe in my "gut feeling," I trust that it has every answer for me. Previous, I was too quick to cast judgment on why others think and do the things they do. But why was that? Why did I worry about things that were not relative to what truly brought me happiness? I created that lifestyle, at times, I now think I created a robotic lifestyle. With social media, busy work lifestyles, always on the go I had foregone the beauty in just taking comfort in just being. Comfort in walking or sitting out in nature and letting my mind, body and soul tell me what feels right for me. Sometimes all I needed was five minutes, other times I needed one hour, but no matter how long it took my walks allowed me to relax, become mindful and present.

"It's a beautiful day
Don't let it get away
It's a beautiful day
Don't let it get away "

-lyrics to Beautiful Day by U2

Chapter 12

Educate yourself

E ducation is important, but what is education? I often wonder
what the true meaning of education really is. A definition I
found online states" the process of receiving or giving systematic
instruction, especially at a school or university" but there is also
another definition that states "an enlightening experience." So
what does education look like for you? Education came in so many
formats for me: attending college, volunteering in areas that I had
a passion for, and in reading.

I read more in this past year then I have in my entire life
put together. Books I had chosen to read primary focused on
inspirational, self-help books and function of the brain. I increased
my awareness on how the brain works and began to understand
my past behaviors, actions and decisions. Each book had a special
meaning to me that I could relate to individually. They also kept
me focused and dedicated in my new direction in life, direction
that continues to lead me in positive changes.

In addition, I have been volunteering this past year and half and
it's incredible how much I've learned. It allowed me to understand
the passion and love in others, become more confident in the

choices I have made recently and develop amazing relationships and connections with individuals that otherwise I would have never had the pleasure to meet. It's truly been a wonderful experience for me to learn and grow from my volunteering experiences.

"The whole world is my cheerleader.
I am brilliant.
Life gives me everything I need.
Oh my God, I'm dong such a fabulous job.
I love how brave I am.
I love how loving I am.
I am majestic."

Part of a prayer from Heart Candy Prayer by
Ford, Debbie. Your Holiness-Discover
the light within. (2018).

Chapter 13

Inspirational quotes

I nspirational quotes were powerful and thought provoking for me. I would take a few moments to myself to understand what each inspirational quote meant. I was mindful, presently aware, of how each quote made me feel at that moment. Some quotes gave me that "pump in my step," gave me the nudge to help get through those difficult days. There were a few that really resonated with me, I wrote them down, read them, visualize them, those quotes would put a smile on my face that sometimes I needed. I have included some of those quotes throughout this book. I found that they helped change my perspective, guided me to the positive direction that sometimes I needed. I hope they do the same for you.

*"If you judge people,
you have no time to
love them."*

- By Mother Teresa

Chapter *14*

Fill yourself with love- stop judgments and assumptions

Judgments and assumptions. We all do it, we make assumptions and we all make judgments. I convinced myself that I didn't take part in judgments, but the reality was, there were times in my life judgments or assumptions were made. This particular one was huge for me, and until recently I didn't know it was. I now understand that many of the negative emotions that I had in various experiences such as fear, anger, and shame, each and every one of them came from my own assumptions. I often assumed things that realistically I had no idea whether they were true and yet I allowed them to consume my mind and my thoughts. Assumptions such as how others felt about me, whether others liked me, or judgments of others simply because of appearances, fashion and/or material things. Those assumptions, those judgments that I created are examples of how conflict occurs. Do you make assumptions? Do you cast judgments? I for one, constantly made assumptions, I look back and I now realize how I would worry myself sick thinking about if I had hurt someone's feelings or caused sleepless nights thinking, "what if's." I judged those who I felt didn't make the right choices in life. I saw them as individuals beneath me at times. How ignorant and foolish of me to think that way. My internal assumptions and judgments caused me stress. I lead myself to believe in things/ideas that I created for no reason at all. I have a different approach now, I don't assume anything, and I don't judge anyone because we are all equal. People, each and every one of us, have a story. Each and every one of us has a different story, that's what makes us unique, that's what makes us beautiful. Judgments, there's no place for them. I don't know where people have been or where they are going, just like they don't know where I have been or where I'm going.

"It's time to see what I can do
To test the limits and break through
No right, no wrong, no rules for me,
I'm free!"

Lyrics from "Let it Go" By Idina Menzel

Chapter 15

Unplug from social media, find a healthy balance

Finding a healthy balance between social media and face-to-face connection is important. In a world where everything is fast paced, on the go and the expectation that we respond instantly, makes it hard to disconnect. We are fortunate to have the Internet at our fingertips for a lot of reasons. We now live in a world where we can communicate with family and friends all over the world, get answers to basically anything we can think of in just a few clicks. We can view pictures of your family and friends and stay connected in seconds, but when do we take a break? When do we stop and just sit and talk to one another. I recognized that social media was far from doing anything good for me at certain times in my life. During these times I would make a choice, to "unplug" as they say now. I quickly realized that as others were talking about things that they had heard on the Internet, pictures they'd seen, events that were happening, all of them were unknown to me. It actually made me realize how much information I received simply from social media. However, at the time it's exactly what I needed. I needed me time. Not social media time, not viewing the latest stories, the latest buzz, or the latest fad diets, etc. I needed me time. Making a choice to "unplug" allowed just that. I have realized removing myself from social media completely doesn't work for me; however, I do make an effort to unplug daily focus on connecting with myself and with others face-to-face. We all need a little connection, affection, and love.

"You don't always need a plan

Sometimes you just need to
Breath, Trust, Let go and
See what happens."

-By Mandy Hale

Chapter *16*

Life isn't all about a plan

Calendars, day timers, schedules. I was that person. I had a plan for everything, how much money I wanted to save, retirement, children's education fund, trips and the list went on and on. In my mind, a plan was what everyone needed. It certainly gave me a direction, it kept me focused and I set goals for myself to achieve those "plans," those "schedules" I created for myself. One thing I learned over the course of the last ten years, life isn't a plan. I believe everyone should plan for there future, I worked in the financial sector for nearly sixteen years, and I certainly see the value in saving for tomorrow. However, there is something about today and just enjoying today. Take a moment and ask yourself what does your plan look like? What does your schedule look like? Does your calendar, your day timer, your schedule look so full of "things" that you have no time for spontaneity? I still have plans, I still like to have some sort of structure; however, now my plans are not "carved in stone." My ife experiences changed my schedule what seemed like in seconds. I am much more open-minded now and accept that "the plan" I set for myself no longer fits my life. Now, I expect plans to change, schedules to change because we as individuals change. I changed based on my life experiences and along that so did my "life plan." My new life plan still involves planning for retirement; however, the memories I create today are far more important and take precedence over any future plans that I once thought may have been the priority.

"What doesn't kill you makes you stronger
Stand a little taller
Doesn't mean I'm lonely when I'm alone
What doesn't kill you makes a fighter
Footsteps even lighter
Doesn't mean I'm over 'cause you're gone."

-Lyrics from Stronger by Kelly Clarkson

Chapter 17

Pets are a gift

Anyone who knows me will find me, talking about pets, shocking! I have to admit for years I had no love for pets. I know to those "pet lovers" (which by the way I am one of you now) I appear to be heartless. I have no idea why I had no desire for animals. I can't even explain it to you today. All I know is that for the first thirty-eight years of my life, I had very little use for animals. But then, my child, after months of nagging, convinced me to get a dog. Thank goodness we did. Our Yorkie Maltese has brought our family so much joy. I can't express how much I love this animal. I look forward to spending time with her while the kids are at school and my husband's at work. I look forward to playing catch, long walks and just cuddle time. She truly adds so much joy to our lives. She was a wonderful surprise and a blessing to us all. Our amazing dog completes our family.

"Strength doesn't come from
what you can do.
It comes from overcoming
The things you once thought
You couldn't."

-By Rikki Rogers

Chapter *18*

Seek professional help

There comes a time when we need professionals. I'm no professional. I just know what worked for me during my life experiences and I hope that some of what I say in this book can help you too. You know your body best, and you know your mind best. When you have moments that you just need a little more support don't hesitate to go get it. There was a couple times in my life when I needed it. There's this stigma that is implied when you go see a counselor or psychiatrist, but in the end we need to stop the stigma. It needs to be that simple, stop the stigma. Seeing a psychiatrist shouldn't be any different than seeing your doctor. If you need to talk to someone, to support you during a difficult time, then welcome it. It's what you deserve. It was incredible how much weight was lifted off my shoulders in just a few short hours. It was worth it, worth putting in the time for me.

I had a friend who once said to me, my psychiatrist hasn't said anything different than what you have and any of my friends have said to me, but something is different when you hear from someone with authority, someone with the accreditation behind them. Maybe, that's just it, someone you don't know, who you don't feel will judge, and will just listen to what you have to say. Listen to your feelings and provide some thoughtful feedback. My advice to you, it never hurts to talk to someone about how you are feeling. You are worth it.

"*Today I decided to forgive you.*
Not because you apologized, or because
You acknowledged the pain that you
Caused me, but because my
Soul deserves peace."

-By Najwa Zebian

Chapter 19

Forgiveness

F orgiveness. My last strategy, certainly not the least important if anything one of the most important. Perhaps, I have left it last because it was the one thing that took me so long to do. Twenty-seven years and I finally forgave my father. Twenty-seven years that I didn't know my body, mind and soul needed to forgive. Twenty-seven years that I held so much pain inside because I needed to forgive.

I can't express this enough, *FORGIVENESS* is for you! I know that you have had your shares of challenges or experiences that the thought of forgiveness might seem like an impossible task. But it's important to forgive. Forgive yourself, forgive the other individual, and forgive their actions. We can't control some of our experiences that we have had, but we can control the anger within us. Anger can become a tornado inside of us, raging and waiting to come out at any given moment that can lead to negative actions. I'm willing to bet, that there is something or someone inside of you that needs forgiveness. Forgiveness can release so much pain. Does this mean you need to attain a relationship with those you have forgiven? No. Does this mean you need to reach out to those who have hurt you? No. Forgive for yourself, so you can move forward for you. Forgive so the pressure that is sitting on your shoulders right now can finally be removed.

Only you can make the decision to forgive. There are many ways that can provide guidance in forgiving yourself and/or others. Myself, I found writing to be extremely helpful, but I also found a book that helped me to where I am today. There are countless books that you can read about forgiveness, the one I read was, "The book of Forgiving: The Fourth Path for Healing Ourselves" by Desmond Tutu and Mpho Andrea Tutu. It was helpful to me.

As I end this book, I will leave you with one more lyric, a song that I find empowering and motivating. A song that made me fight when I thought I had no more fight in me.

"This is my fight song
Take back my life song
Prove I'm alright song
My power's turned on
Starting right now I'll be strong
I'll play my fight song
And I don't really care if nobody else believes
'Cause I've still got a lot of fight left in me."

-Lyrics from Fight Song by Rachel Platten

Everyday is a gift, live life to its fullest. God Bless.

Acknowledgements

To my friends and extended family, thank you, for always being a part of my life. Through highs, lows and everything in between each of you have supported me in your own special way.

To the many individuals who have supported me at different times in my life, I will forever be grateful for the love, compassion, and kindness you provided me, thank you. Each of you provided me a step to get me to where I am today, thank you.

To the people who knew when I needed support, a shoulder to cry on, a journal to write, learn the power in the word "yet" and the importance in a gentle touch when I needed it most, thank you. You gave me the courage and motivation to keep going on this journey. You all know who you are, thank you for being you.

Thank you to those who didn't believe in me or thought I was making wrong decisions in life. You helped me fight harder, you helped me realize the amount of strength I had inside when I needed it most. That strength and fight lead me to achieve my goals in life. Thank you.

Thank you to my fitness trainer and yoga instructor. I will forever be grateful; the both of you helped me both mentally and physically. You helped me more than you will ever know, thank you.

Thank you to the people who took the time to read my very "rough " drafts. Each of you provided me very helpful feedback and allowed me to better myself and discover the beauty in writing.

Thank you to the healthcare providers who devote their lives in improving the health of others. I have had the pleasure of meeting and working together with some of you. Thank you for your dedication, commitment and love in improving our healthcare system.

Thank you to the all who took part in making what I had to say into my first book. Feedbacks, revisions, cover pictures, editing and publishing without your support, ideas and suggestions this would never have become a reality.

To my amazing, wonderful and beautiful family, my life is whole because of you. You are my everything. Each of you amazes me with your strength, love, kindness, passion and commitment. Your support during this journey has meant everything to me. I love you all.

Lightning Source UK Ltd.
Milton Keynes UK
UKHW01n1859020818
326695UK00001B/3/P